Periods for Young Girls

9 Proven Strategies for Confidently Navigating the Menstrual Cycle, Celebrating Puberty, and Practicing Self-Care and Body Acceptance for Growing Tweens

Carly Gross

Table of Contents

Introduction

"You have been criticizing yourself for years, and it hasn't worked. Try approving of yourself and see what happens."
Louise Hay

Will I be ready? What will it feel like? What if it happens at school or somewhere totally unexpected?

Have you been imagining what it will be like getting your first period? Maybe you've heard whispers about periods and wondered, *What's this fuss about?* Perhaps you've seen a friend carrying a small pouch containing period essentials, and the idea of getting your period makes you curious, excited, and a little nervous.

Well, if you can relate to any of these thoughts, you aren't alone. Many other girls have had similar questions, so there is nothing to be ashamed or scared of.

Having a period is completely normal; it's a sign that your body is working well and you're fully becoming a woman. Though it might seem like a mystery right now, with the right information, guidance, and preparation, you'll soon see that there's nothing to worry about.

You've probably sat with your friends, and suddenly they started talking about periods. At that moment, everyone seems to be in the know, but you, on the other hand, are unsure of what to say because you've not had yours yet or don't know what happens when it starts. So, you would rather keep mute and avoid getting embarrassed.

What if I tell you that you no longer need to feel awkward in such scenarios? With this book, you can have all the right answers to questions about having a period, and you'll be well prepared for when you have yours. This book serves as a guide that will answer all your questions about getting your period and even those you haven't thought of yet.

To be clear, nothing is embarrassing about getting periods, and it shouldn't be a topic to whisper about. Period is a natural and incredible part of growing up, and there's so much power in understanding your body. Every adult girl you've seen does get their period, and they get on with life, feeling strong. You aren't an exception; you too can be a strong, smart girl, ready for whatever comes.

Thankfully, this book will serve as your ultimate guide to confidently navigate the menstrual cycle and embrace the changes your body is about to go through.

This book provides 9 proven strategies to help you navigate your period confidently and embrace the changes your body undergoes during puberty.

Each chapter will discuss one of these strategies, providing you with the right knowledge, support, and tools at every stage.

We'll start with discussing how your body works, showing what to expect when your first period arrives and uncovering stuff no one talks about—the feelings and emotions accompanying your cycle. The final strategies entail discovering fun ways to take care of yourself and learning why it's so important to celebrate your unique body.

Each of the nine strategies will help you grow into the amazing girl that you are, arming you with the right confidence to face obstacles during this puberty stage.

I'm passionate about writing this book because I know what it's like to be in your shoes. As a growing tween, I was curious, unsure, and full of questions about getting my period. I know talking about periods can sometimes feel awkward and maybe a bit embarrassing, so I created the book I wish I could have read. This book is all about YOU. With it, you can navigate puberty and manage your period well.

The changes your body will undergo are natural, and every part of you is worthy of celebration, so don't be harsh on yourself. This book will help you develop self-love and encourage you to celebrate your beautiful body.

You've got this! Your period is just one part of your amazing journey, and no matter where or when it happens, you'll be ready.

Excited for what's coming? Let's get started!

Chapter One
Knowing Your Body

"We are a gorgeous, infinite circle of women of all shades, all styles, in all the ways we were made, inside of us everything blooms."
Alicia Keys

Have you ever been on a journey but didn't know where you were going, even though everyone else seemed as if *they* knew? You are seated in the car, looking terrified as the car moves. You see new things by the road but don't know what they are, and maybe you're too scared to ask anyone. You feel awkward and confused.

The strange feeling you get from such a scenario is similar to how your body now feels to you. Perhaps you look in the mirror and see things about yourself that weren't there before, and it's all so new, confusing, and awkward. Your nipples now have small lumps in them, your face is oilier, your jeans are getting tighter, and maybe you're now bleeding so that now you have to wear thick pads to school.

I know how scary these changes can feel because I've been there before, but trust me, it's nothing to worry about. The changes you're experiencing are a result of a part of life called puberty.

Puberty is a stage of life that you must pass through; it's the beginning of adulthood. Every girl who is an adult has gone through it. So, it's normal and just a phase.

You may wonder, *Why must I go through it?* You'll get your answer soon.

Do you remember when you were a baby—when you were so little and didn't have any teeth? You couldn't walk, talk, or read a book, either. Look at yourself now and compare the changes from that time to now.

Now, you are no longer little, and you have teeth. You can walk, talk, and read, which means you can do the things you couldn't do before. This could be endless if I wanted to make a list of such changes.

The point is that you have to go through these changes. You can't remain a little girl for life; you must grow, and growth doesn't happen overnight. It's a gradual process that gives you a newer version of yourself.

Remember when you were three or maybe five, and your milk teeth fell out only to be replaced by a stronger set of teeth? Each tooth was painful before it fell out, right? Puberty is just like that time. Yes, some of these changes can be painful, but trust your body to do amazingly well.

This chapter will focus on discussing puberty—what it is, how it starts, and what you need to know about your body's anatomy.

What Is Puberty and How Does It Start?

Puberty is the changes that your body experiences during your transition from childhood to adulthood. It's different for everybody, and it typically occurs between the ages of eight and fifteen.

Puberty is not limited to girls. It happens to boys as well, but our focus is on girls.

Puberty starts with gradual changes to your body, and these changes are triggered with the help of hormones. Hormones aid in the success of puberty.

The two primary hormones required for female puberty are estrogen and progesterone. Your brain alerts the ovaries to produce them once you reach the right age. These special hormones, estrogen and progesterone, are responsible for all the physical changes you would experience.

What's Happening to You?

Knowing what to expect is necessary so you can appreciate your body's work. Here, I'd like to take you through the changes your body experiences during puberty so you understand them better and they don't feel strange anymore.

Let me begin with the physical changes. These are the changes that you can see and feel. They include:

- **Development of Breasts**
Breast development is also known as thelarche. At first, you will feel small, slightly painful lumps under your nipples. These lumps will slowly grow into breasts, and this happens because of the changes in your hormones.

Every adult woman has breasts that developed on their own at different stages when they were girls just like you.

As a young girl, this development can be unpleasant and awkward as the stages progress.

These are the stages of breast development in tween girls like you:

- **Stage 1**: The breasts are flat in this stage, and the nipples are slightly raised.
- **Stage 2**: Small breast buds are formed under the nipples (areola). The level of estrogen in your body increases in this stage.
- **Stage 3**: The breasts are more elevated, and the areola enlarges and becomes darker.
- **Stage 4**: The areola and nipple form a secondary mound on top of the developing breast tissue, becoming more obvious.
- **Stage 5**: The breasts are fully grown in this stage.

Breasts usually grow when you are between eight and fifteen years old. You might need to wear bras to support your breasts as they get bigger. There are different types of bras, so you should have fun selecting the ones you like.

Now that you understand how breasts are formed, let's discuss the other changes.

• Body Hair
You might notice hair growing in your armpits when you raise your arm and in your pubic area. This is natural; everybody develops hair like this.

These hairs are slightly thick, and they grow quite fast. The hairs under your arm could cause odor if you don't care for them well because during puberty you'll sweat more. Bathing regularly and using deodorant helps to reduce the odor caused by increased sweating.

• Skin Changes
Your oil glands become more active due to hormone production. This oil makes your face shinier, rougher, and more sensitive. You might also begin to spot acne on your face. You don't need to be scared when you see this.

Acne happens when the pores in your skin are blocked because your skin produces too much oil, but you can control it with proper skincare.

● **Body Changes**

You might start to outgrow your clothes because your body is changing quickly. You might grow taller, your hips could get wider, or you may gain some weight. These happen because of your genes, what you eat, and your hormones. Your friends would look different from you but don't be surprised, as every girl is unique in her changes.

● **Menstruation**

This is the biggest change you will experience. You might wake up one day and see your underwear stained with blood. What's happening to you is called menstruation, or your period.

Your first period is called Menarche. Menarche is different for every girl. It typically starts between the ages of eight and fifteen. It may seem messy and frustrating, but it's still part of the puberty experience. I'll be discussing more about menstruation as we progress.

So far, I've shared the physical changes you will experience. They don't happen at the same time for every girl, so don't be afraid if you haven't started noticing any changes yet. You will go through them eventually, but it's good that you are learning about them now.

The other changes you will experience are emotional. These are the changes that occur in your brain. You can't see them, so they are very different from the physical changes. These include:

- **Mood Swings**

I remember when I started experiencing this. One moment, I would be happy, and the next, very sad, and I would wish to be alone. My older sister informed my mom about my latest on-and-off behavior toward her, and my mom explained what mood swings were to me.

As you grow older, your hormones are changing with you, and your mood might start to swing in a way that you don't like. One moment, you may be happy; the next, you could be sad or angry. These are called mood swings.

Your body is just getting used to the hormones produced, and this may be overwhelming. It's also a phase in puberty. You will get used to all these changes as you grow older.

- **Increased Sensitivity**

As your body changes, you become more aware of the world around you and *its* changes. You may begin to feel offended and lose your temper more than you normally would. This is a phase that is essential for your development.

You may begin to notice how people look at you and your behavior. You may become uncomfortable with certain aspects of your life and find you're increasingly aware of your body as puberty begins. Just remember that this phase will help build your resilience and confidence.

Your mood and sensitivity are vital parts of adulthood, and you are beginning to experience them. You are a strong girl, and I know that you've got this.

Are These Changes Normal?

Yes, the changes you're experiencing are very normal. Your emotions might be messing with you, and you may feel these emotions all at once. You may feel constantly tired and hungry. You might be uncomfortable with how your face and body look, and the idea of bleeding every month might seem weird to you right now.

Whatever your experience is, know that:

- **You Are Not Alone**

Every adult has had a similar experience, and look at them now; they are living great lives. This shows you that it's not a permanent experience, and you will overcome it.

When you feel uncomfortable, you should talk to your parents, an older sibling, a trusted friend, or a teacher. They have also gone through the experience and understand it better.

- **It's Okay to Be Confused**

You might wake up one morning and look in the mirror but not recognize the person you see. It can feel weird for you, and it's okay to admit this. You don't need to act as if you understand what is happening. The truth is, you don't. I was like you, and I was just as confused. It took help from adults for me to feel comfortable and safe.

Just wanting to read this book shows that you are a champion already, so don't be mad at yourself for asking questions. If you don't ask questions, you won't understand what your body is going through. I applaud your efforts in seeking knowledge and understanding.

It's okay if you don't know exactly what you're experiencing. This is why you should speak with someone. They will help you navigate through this phase. Know that with time, you can manage your emotions better and be more comfortable in your skin.

● Puberty Is a Sign of Growth

Puberty is a sign of growth and a transition into adulthood. It shows that your body is preparing you for adulthood. It's also a sign of good health.

You're on a journey. It is okay to be confused and to seek support. These changes indicate a healthy body doing what it is designed to do.

● Everyone Is Different

Raise a hand and observe your five fingers. What do you notice? They're all fingers, but have you ever wondered why they are of different lengths and sizes?

As humans, none of us are the same, just as our fingers aren't the same. It's what makes us special and unique. We come in different shapes, sizes, and forms, making us special. While some of us are short, others are tall or slim. Some have gorgeous kinky curls, while others have long, smooth hair. Every difference is worth celebrating.

● Embrace Your Difference

Don't shy away from your changes. Remember that humans are not all the same, and that's normal! Don't let all the drama going on in your head make you think you are not special. Of course, you are! Look at you—you are beautiful and going through puberty.

Your body is perfectly made, and you should be proud of that. Your difference is what makes you who you are. Look at your body and admire your differences.

- **The Timeline of Puberty Is Different for Everyone**

Some of your friends are getting taller, and some have started their periods, but you haven't started yours yet.

If that's your experience, don't be sad. Everyone has a timeline that can't be rushed. You can only wait for your turn to come. It doesn't mean that something is wrong with you. It only shows that there is no wrong or right time. However, you should talk to someone if you are over 15 years old and there are no signs of puberty.

- **Focus on the Uniqueness of Your Body**

Your body is going through many changes to transition smoothly into adulthood, and that's something to be proud of. Focus on how well your brain and body are working and appreciate them.

Don't compare yourself to others because it would take away from the experience. Comparison is nothing but a thief of joy. Remember that!

Understanding your body is essential at this stage of your life. Focus on your body and learn what it can do. Your body has many special processes going on, and you should know about them.

Understanding Your Body's Anatomy

Your body is doing cool work and has systems that do different things to keep you healthy. One of the many systems is the female reproductive system. This system is unique in what it does, and I will explain why.

The female reproductive system is a complex organ structure that works together to help your body through puberty, menstruation, and childbirth.

It consists of external and internal parts.

The external part is called the vulva, and it consists of the labia majora, the labia minora, the clitoris, the hymen, and the vaginal opening. These are the parts that you can see.

The internal part is the part that you can't see. It consists of:

- The vagina connects the external part to the uterus, and it is also the birth canal. This means that babies pass through the canal to come into this world.

- The cervix keeps the uterus enclosed and protected, which makes it a very important part.

- The uterus, or the womb, is where a fertilized egg grows into a baby. If the egg is not fertilized, it sheds its thickened lining, which causes your period.

- The fallopian tube is the road the egg travels to reach the uterus. You have two of them.

- There are two ovaries as well. This part produces the eggs and the two special hormones we discussed earlier, which are the most active during puberty and menstruation.

Your body is so amazing, and knowing how it works should make you more confident in its abilities. The changes you undergo are normal, and you should be proud of yourself.

This chapter discussed knowing your body and what's happening to you, embracing the changes, and understanding your reproductive system. The next chapter will focus on the menstrual cycle and you. Stay with me!

Chapter Two
The Menstrual Cycle and You

"Menstruation is not a curse, it is a gift that allows us to connect with our bodies and the earth in a profound way."
Period Power

Your body is so amazing! It does so many awesome things to make you healthy and happy. Every day, you breathe, eat, sleep, run, and think, all because of the organs in your body. And guess what? The menstrual cycle is just one of those awesome things your body handles.

What comes to your mind when you hear "menstrual cycle?" Are you thinking about bicycles and tricycles? Well, don't be like me.

When I was younger, I thought the menstrual cycle meant wheels or bikes when I first heard the word. But I was wrong. This type of cycle is about your body. It's when your body gets ready for something special every month.

This monthly prep stage is entirely natural; every girl goes through it. It's a sign that your body is healthy and strong. However, even though your body is doing all this prep work, that doesn't mean a change must happen immediately. Most of the time, your body is just practicing and getting used to a routine.

It's like when you read your books. That doesn't necessarily mean you're preparing for a test that'll happen tomorrow. Maybe you want to be ready in case you need it. Your body does something similar during the menstrual cycle.

Now, if all this sounds like big science words, don't worry. In this chapter, you'll learn more about what your body is preparing for and why that's such an essential part of growing up.

What Is a Menstrual Cycle?

"Menstrual" is just a fancy word for something that happens once a month. Think of it as how your parents work throughout the month and get paid at the end—it's a monthly thing!

"Cycle" is a word that means something that goes around and around. It's like the way every week starts with Monday and ends with Sunday, only to begin again.

Put "menstrual" and "cycle" together, and you get the "menstrual cycle"—an event that happens once a month, every month.

During the menstrual cycle, your body is getting ready to

act in case you want to have a baby. Your body is preparing a soft, comfy space where a baby can grow, even though that won't happen until later. Your body practices this every month to stay ready.

I remember one afternoon when I was in my room studying and my mom came to the door. She had a smile on her face. That smile usually meant one of two things: either she had a surprise waiting for me, or she was about to have one of those scolding sessions. Spoiler alert—it wasn't a scolding session!

She said we needed to talk. She mentioned the menstrual cycle but I didn't understand. This wasn't the surprise I had hoped for. So, I asked mom for further explanation.

My mom explained how my body was preparing itself for something important. As she talked, she showed me a calendar and pointed out how my body would follow a monthly schedule. Usually, it would clean up and start fresh for the next cycle. The entire explanation sounded strange.

Did you feel this way when you first heard the word "menstrual cycle?" Did you feel scared and uncomfortable? Well, you don't need to be. I'll tell you all you need to know about this beautiful process.

Imagine you're getting ready for a school play or a dance show. You wouldn't just go on stage without practicing first. You'd rehearse your lines or dance moves to ensure everything is perfect before the big day. Your body does something similar with the menstrual cycle!

Every month, your body gets ready for a possible big event. In this way, your body is practicing how to have a baby in the future. Don't worry, you don't need a baby now, but you probably will many years from now. That's what your body is preparing for.

Most of the time, there's no baby to grow, so your body says, *Okay, we practiced, but the show isn't happening this time.* Then, it cleans up the stage and prepares for the next practice, your next menstrual cycle.

This practice happens every month. So, your body stays prepared, just in case. It's your body's way of making sure everything is ready. So, when the time is right for it to grow a baby, it'll be all set for the big event! And that's what the menstrual cycle is!

During the menstrual cycle, you might notice new feelings in your body. For example, you might feel a bit of a tummy ache or sharp pain in your lower belly. This is just your body getting ready. It'll only last for a couple of days before it disappears.

You might also feel more tired than usual. You may need extra rest. You might also get more emotional. Sometimes, you'd feel sad, grumpy, or upset about things that usually wouldn't bother you. When all these happen, don't be scared. This is just another part of the cycle. And it happens because of the changes going on inside your body.

Phases of the Cycle

We've talked so much about what the menstrual cycle means. Now, we'll discuss the menstrual cycle phases and what happens in each phase.

The menstrual cycle is divided into four phases, and with each one, something new happens. We'll find out what those are soon.

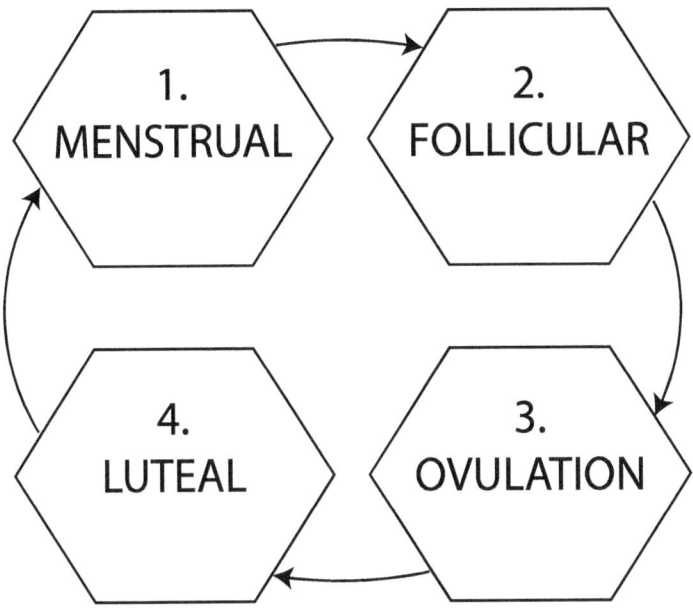

Think of your body as a garden. It's a beautiful garden with different colorful flowers. Your garden goes through four different seasons every month to prepare for the possibility of growing another beautiful flower.

These four seasons start with the cleanup stage (menstrual phase) and go on to the seed planting stage (follicular phase), then the garden party (ovulation), and lastly, the resting stage (luteal phase). All four phases must happen for the menstrual cycle to be complete.

● **Phase 1: Menstrual Phase**
Every good garden needs a fresh start. So, at the beginning of the month, your garden decides it's time for some serious cleaning. It's like when you want to plant a new flower—you discard all the old leaves and dry flowers from last month's work.

This is what happens when your body has its period. Your body decides it doesn't need those dry leaves, so it starts to clean up. Sure, it might be messy, but it's all part of getting ready for a new season.

There's a part of every girl's tummy called the uterus. It's the warm, cozy part where a baby grows. Since you're not ready to have a baby, your uterus gets rid of its old lining because it's time to start afresh. That's what leads to your period. The blood you see is that old lining coming out because it's no longer needed. This phase usually lasts about 3 to 7 days.

● Phase 2: Follicular Phase

Once the garden is all tidy and clean, it's time to start planting the seeds. But not just any seed. You need the best seed that'll give you beautiful flowers.

In your stomach, you have organs called ovaries that produce the seeds that will be planted in your garden. During the follicular phase, your body carefully prepares the uterus. It ensures that it's nice and soft in case the egg settles in. Your brain then signals to your ovaries to prepare for a new cycle. The ovaries prepare a little egg inside a tiny sac called a follicle.

The follicular phase starts on the first day of your period and lasts until ovulation, about ten to fourteen days.

● Phase 3: Ovulation

And now, the moment for the big garden party! During ovulation, your garden is throwing a big party. This is when the seed is released into the soil, and everything in the garden is ready to grow.

Your body is like the host of the party. It makes sure everything is just right for the big event. When the selected egg is fully ready and released from the ovary, it travels down a tube called the fallopian tube in your abdomen. Then, it's ready to be fertilized.

If your egg meets a sperm (boy's egg) during this time, it might start growing into a baby. But if not, it waits a bit and then moves on. Ovulation usually happens around the middle of your cycle, about fourteen days before your next period.

● **Phase 4: Luteal Phase**

Now, if the seed doesn't start growing into a flower, the garden knows it's time to take a little break. The party's over, and the garden needs to rest up for next month's cycle. This is the luteal phase, where your body breathes and reflects on all the hard work it's done.

It's like when you finish a big project and are ready to chill out for a while. The garden might still look nice and tidy, but it knows it's almost time to start the process again. This phase is the last 14 days leading up to your period.

And then, the cycle resets and begins anew! Every month, your garden goes through these fantastic phases. It works hard to create the perfect conditions for your seed. Each phase must do its part for the menstrual cycle to be complete.

Imagine if you were baking a cake, but you skipped some steps. You might not have mixed the batter well because you ran out of time. Would the cake turn out right? Probably not! The same thing happens with the menstrual cycle.

Each of the four phases is like a step in a recipe. First, your body prepares by growing a soft lining in your uterus. Then, an egg is released. If that egg isn't needed, your body clears everything out during your period to start fresh. Skipping any of these would be like trying to bake that cake without mixing the batter—it just wouldn't work!

Why Does Menstruation Happen?

Let's talk about why this all matters. Why does your body go through this cycle every month? What's the point of all this planning and preparing, especially when you're not even considering having a baby right now? Why does your body do all of this when you're only a child?

Well, the menstrual cycle isn't just about having babies. Your menstrual cycle is a sign that your body is growing, developing, and working exactly as it should.

Right now, it might seem like a lot of work for something that isn't happening yet, but your body is smart. It wants to be ready for anything and keeps things in order. Every month, practice gets everything in shape just in case, one day far in the future, you decide you want to have a baby.

Even though it might feel strange right now, having a menstrual cycle is a sign that your body is fantastic. It shows that you're getting stronger and healthier as you become an adult. It's one of the many ways your body shows how good it is at caring for you.

And guess what? Even though it might seem like a big deal, your body handles it all on its own. You don't have to think about it or do anything special—it just happens! This is thanks to hormones, which handle all the tasks.

Even though you can't see them, these hormones are always busy behind the scenes. They're making sure everything runs smoothly.

So, while you spend your day playing, learning, and having fun, your hormones are hard at work. They're working hard to ensure your body stays healthy and ready for whatever comes next!

Two of the most important hormones involved in your menstrual cycle are estrogen and progesterone.

Estrogen starts working early in the menstrual cycle. Its job is to help build up the uterus lining (the inside of the cozy room we discussed earlier).

Progesterone comes in after estrogen is done building the lining of the uterus. It makes the space extra cozy and makes the lining even thicker, softer, and super comfy for the egg.

Now, if an egg comes along and needs a place to stay, the lining is all ready for it. But if no egg shows up, your body decides it's time to clean up and start over. When this happens, the levels of estrogen and progesterone drop. The lining then breaks down and comes out of your body as your period.

I know all this new information might feel weird and even confusing, but remember, you're not alone! Every girl goes through this. We all face similar experiences.

So, when your body starts changing, and you notice signs of the menstrual cycle, remember that we all experience it. It's like a big secret that connects girls and women all over the world.

Do you remember my story about my mom telling me about periods? Honestly, I didn't understand everything she told me at first. All the new terms about how my body would change made me worried. I wondered why this had to happen and if I was ready for it.

It wasn't just the big words that upset me—it was the idea of something new coming into my life. I felt like I was going to bleed out a river when my period started.

Seeing how I was feeling, my mom sat beside me. She put her arm around me and gave me a comforting hug. My mom shared stories about when she first learned about periods. She told me that although it might be confusing initially, it was just a normal part of growing up.

My mom explained that every girl goes through it, which signifies that I'm becoming a big girl. She shared her feelings from when she was my age and ensured I knew there was no rush. We could discuss it as much as I wanted and figure things out together.

What helped me feel better was how she made everything seem normal. We even found funny videos and stories about how other women handled their periods. These made me laugh and feel more at ease.

By the end of our conversation, I felt a lot better. My mom had turned something that felt scary and confusing into something I looked forward to. If you ever feel worried or unsure about anything, remember it's okay to ask questions and talk about it. You're never alone; there's always someone who can help you understand and feel better.

This journey is something millions of girls have gone through before, and millions more will go through it after you. So, no matter what, there are lots of girls out there who understand exactly what you're going through. And as you keep learning about your body and its beauty, you'll see how strong you are.

This chapter is only a tiny slice of the large cake I have for you. There's still much to learn. In the next chapter, we'll talk about getting your periods. Yes! I'll tell you all there is to know about getting your first period. So, don't stay away for too long. I'll be waiting for you on the next page.

Carly Gross

Chapter Three
Getting Your First Period

"Each individual woman's body demands to be accepted on its own terms."
Gloria Steinem

So, let's talk about getting your period.

I know you're thinking, *Eww, blood*, but it's not so bad. Getting your period isn't scary; it's not something to worry about. Just think of it as your body saying, "You're a big girl now" or "Let's get all that baby blood out and put some fresh big girl blood in you."

So, you don't need to feel weird or get upset. It's a normal thing that comes and goes. And you're not the only one who gets a period. Every girl does! I want you to know that getting your first period is a time for you to learn about your body—checking out the things you're comfortable with, the things you're not, and what food your body likes. It's a great time to discover yourself all over again.

In this chapter, I'll tell you everything you need to prepare for your first period. We'll talk about everything here, even the happy times and the not-so-happy times. When you're done reading, I'm sure you'll be excited about getting your first period. All you'll learn here will prepare you for the beautiful journey ahead!

What to Expect

Getting my first period was one of the most anticipated moments of my life! Having had my mom explain all the processes to me, I was already eager to get my period and truly feel what this entailed. All my friends at school had started to get their periods, but not me! It felt like my body was holding me back and telling me to keep waiting.

When all the girls were talking about their periods, I couldn't join in the conversation because I hadn't gotten mine yet. So, you can imagine the joy I felt when I started getting signs that my first period was on its way!

I had a pink dress that my mom got me for my birthday. I loved it so much that I would have liked to wear it every day of the week. It easily became my favorite dress. But when I wore it one morning, it felt too tight around my chest. I looked in the mirror and saw that my breasts were starting to grow.

Then, the next week, I had some very weird cravings. Oh, they were so wild! I wanted to eat anything and everything. I loved peanut butter and jelly sandwiches but suddenly wanted pickles with chocolate sauce. Yes, pickles and chocolate! I tried the pickle and chocolate combo, and even though it was a bit strange, it made me happy.

During that time, I also got a few pimples on my face. The acne hurt a lot, but I got over it in time. Not only that, but my tummy also started feeling a bit different. It wasn't painful, but something strange was happening there.

Sometimes, I'd get so tired that all I wanted to do was sleep. I'd get home and hop in bed for a long nap. Other times, I'd be so full of energy that I would do all my chores immediately after I got home from school.

All these funny signs were clues telling me that my first period was on its way, and I was so excited. When it finally happened, I was ready for it! My body had been giving me all the hints and helping me prepare, so I wasn't too surprised.

Have you been seeing the signs lately? Did your clothes get too small, and is your face now more rounded? If yes, these are possibly signs that your period is coming soon. However, you don't need to worry if you *don't* get these signs. There's nothing wrong with you!

Every girl's body is different. So, my body might show me some signs and show you a different set of signs. It doesn't mean you won't get your period, and it also doesn't mean that your body is slow. You need to pay close attention to what your body is saying and take its cues.

Some cues you could notice when your period is coming are:

- **Stomach cramps**
One of the first signs you'll feel is cramping in your lower tummy. It might feel like a gentle tug or a dull ache. If you've ever had a muscle cramp in your leg or arm, you know that sudden, uncomfortable feeling.

Stomach cramps feel like a gentle but persistent ache in your lower stomach, lower back, or even hips. They tend to linger a bit, so they don't disappear as quickly as a leg cramp might.

When you feel these cramps, it's a pretty good hint that your first period could arrive within the next day or two. This cramping is your body's way of getting ready for your period.

A warm heating pad or a hot water bottle on your lower tummy can help you feel better. The heat from the bottle helps relax the muscles. If you don't have a heating pad, a warm bath can help, too. You can also drink a lot of water and take some pain relievers to reduce the pain.

- **Breast changes**

Usually, your breasts start growing and then your first period comes one or two years later. So, once your clothes start becoming tight at the chest, know that your period is close.

When your breasts start changing, you might feel a bit of soreness or pain. Even a slight touch will hurt. Don't be afraid! Remember those hormones we talked about in the last chapter? They're responsible for this breast pain.

What can you do to help yourself ease the pain? Use a warm or cold cloth to massage your breasts. It might hurt a little, so you don't want to go hard. Massage it softly and slowly.

If you've already started wearing a bra, getting a well-fitted one will also support you and reduce the pain. Wearing a sports bra can help because it keeps your breasts from moving around too much. When they stay stable, you won't feel the pain as much.

- **Skin problems (oily skin, acne, eczema)**

If you've never had acne and you suddenly wake up with a pimple, that might be a sign that your period is close. It could also be a part of growing up. It's a bit tricky to tell right at the beginning. But as you have more periods, you'll notice a pattern in your skin changes.

A lot of girls find that their skin breaks out about a week or two before their period. So, even if you're using special face washes, you might still get a few pimples during this time. It doesn't mean your skin products aren't working. It just means that your skin is now more sensitive.

You can manage these skin problems by drinking lots of water, washing your face with mild face washes, and keeping your bedsheet and pillowcases clean. You should also avoid touching your face with dirty hands because this can pass germs on.

• Vaginal discharges

About a year before you start your period, you might see a discharge in your underwear. This is normal! It doesn't mean you're unclean or ill. At first, the discharge will be thin and look a little clear or whitish, just like a jelly.

As time passes, the discharge might start looking like egg whites. It'll get slippery and stretchy. When you notice this, it's a sign that your period might be just a few weeks away.

Some girls don't see any discharge in the week before their period starts, and that's fine. Everyone is different. So, if you don't notice this discharge, you're okay. To manage this discharge, wash your panties and sundry them properly before wearing them again.

• More pubic and armpit hair

As you grow older, hair starts to grow in your armpit and also in your private areas. But as your period gets closer, you'll notice that this hair becomes fuller. The hair starts spreading out more than before. It becomes thicker and more noticeable. When this happens, start preparing because your period is close.

The body changes, increase in height, and tiredness might seem a bit strange at first, but they're all normal. With time, you'll get used to having them around. These signs don't mean you're ill or weird, they're your body's way of telling you to prepare for your period.

Preparing for the Big Day

When I was the last one in my group of friends still waiting to get her period, it made me feel left out sometimes.

One day, my mom invited me to shop with her for period stuff. She wanted to pick out some pads, period panties, and other things she needed. I was really curious.

We went to the store, and I couldn't believe how many options there were. The shelves were packed with many things, and some packages were super cute. There were pads in bright pink boxes—some in beautiful colors and even some with little flowers.

I couldn't believe how pretty these products looked. It was almost like shopping for new school supplies, but way more fun. We made jokes about picking the ones that matched our outfits!

My mom showed me how she chose her pads. She said that some were longer for nighttime and others smaller for daytime. Some pads had wings, which she said helped them stay in place. Others were super thin but still did the job. I asked her a million questions about how they worked, and she answered them. We even joked about how pads looked like mini diapers.

We also found period panties—I didn't even know they existed! They came in so many colors. We picked out some together, and I imagined how cool it would be when I could shop for mine.

As we kept shopping, we found heat patches that you could stick on your stomach to help with cramps.

When we left the store, my curiosity had turned into excitement. I couldn't wait to start my period so I could do my special shopping.

Many girls get confused when it's time to choose a period product. They're worried because there are so many period products to pick from, and they all look so pretty. But I'm here to help you. I'll tell you what these period products are and what they do so you can choose the ones that are best for you.

Here are the types of period products and how to use them.

● Pads

Pads go in your underwear to catch the blood when your period starts. They're soft on one side and sticky on the other side. The sticky side helps your pad stay glued to your underwear. The other side of the pad is made of a unique material that soaks up the blood during your period.

A lot of girls use pads when they first start their period because they're really easy to use. If your period is heavy, you might use a thicker pad; if it's light, a thinner one will do the job.

There are also pantyliners—smaller, thinner types of pads. Pantyliners are great for days when your period is very light or for extra protection.

You should change your pad every four to six hours to stay fresh and clean. When you're ready to change it, don't flush it down the toilet. Instead, wrap it in toilet paper and throw it in the trash.

● Tampons

Tampons are tiny, soft tubes made of cotton. You put them inside your vagina, and they absorb the blood from your period before it comes out of your body. Once the tampon is in, your vagina holds it snugly in place.

In case you're wondering if the tampon would get lost in your vagina, no, it won't! A string at the end of the tampon stays outside your body, and you use it to pull the tampon out when it's time to change it.

Tampons usually come with instructions that show you how to use them. So, if you've put it in correctly, you shouldn't feel it at all. But if it hurts, it means it's not in the right spot, and you should try again.

There are different types of tampons. Some are made for lighter periods and others for heavier ones. You can tell which is which by looking at the packaging. It will say if it's for light, medium, or heavy periods. Always make sure you take out your tampon every four to six hours!

● Period pants

These are special underwear made for periods. They're just like regular underwear but special because they absorb menstrual blood just as pads or tampons do!

Period pants are very comfortable because you can wash them and use them again. You'll need to wear them every day during your period. So, you need to have enough pairs to always have a clean one ready. When you're done wearing them for the day, you can wash and dry them, and they'll be fresh and ready to wear again.

Apart from these period products, you'll need other important things. The following are period essentials and their uses.

- **The period kit**

A period kit is a small, cute bag with all your period products. You carry it with you just in case your period starts when you're not at home. It must be super handy and safe. Just as you find your books and pens in a school bag, you'll find your pads and tampons in a period kit.

- **Hand sanitizer**

The hand sanitizer in a period kit helps keep your hands clean when changing your pad or tampon. This is especially important when you don't have easy access to soap and water. After you've touched your pad or tampon, you can use a little hand sanitizer to ensure your hands are nice and clean.

- **Wipes or tissues**

Wipes and tissues also help you stay clean. Wipes are gentle, moist cloths that help you feel fresh and remove any blood on your skin. They're handy when you're not at home or have no bathroom access.

You can use tissue to dry off after using a wipe. It's also helpful in wrapping up your used pad or tampon before you throw it in the trash. This helps keep everything neat.

- **Extra underwear**

Sometimes, your pad or tampon might get wet quickly. You'd need to change underwear so you can feel comfortable. This is why it's always a great idea to have an extra pair of underwear in your period kit.

Once you have all these period essentials, you'll do fine when your period comes. But I won't leave you just like that. I will tell you what to do when you get your first period.

When your first period comes, you'll notice some reddish or brownish stains on your panties. Don't freak out, okay? That means your first period has started.

First things first—take a deep breath. It's no big deal. You can do this on your own, but if you don't feel confident doing it independently, find your mom, an older sister, or another female adult you feel comfortable with. Let them know what's happening. They've all been through this, and they'll know exactly how to help you.

Next, you'll need a pad. Pads are super easy to use. If your underwear got a little messy, no worries! Just grab a clean pair. Ensure you change your pads every four to six hours. Don't leave them on for too long!

Now that you've started your period, carrying a little period kit is smart. As discussed earlier, pop a few pads, wipes, and a spare pair of underwear into a small bag and keep it in your backpack or locker. Don't be shy if you're confused or curious about anything—ask away!

Sometimes, you might have a tiny tummy ache. That's normal. Just rest, drink water, and sleep. And that's it! You're all set. But if you can't manage the pain, you can ask for pain meds to help you.

Understanding Period Length and Tracking Your Cycle

Your period length is the number of days in which menstrual blood escapes from your vagina. For most girls, periods come once every month. But it doesn't always fall on the same date every single month. So, here's the scoop—when your period starts, it usually lasts about three to seven days. It might be a bit shorter or longer, and that's normal!

At first, your period might be unpredictable, so settling into a regular pattern could take a few months. But there's something cool you can do to keep track of your period.

Every time your period starts, you can mark it on a calendar, in a special notebook, or even use a period app if you like! Write down the first day of your period and how many days it lasts. This way, you'll start to see how long your periods are and figure out when your next one might come.

Now, let's talk about tracking your cycle. Tracking your period means keeping a diary about what your body is doing each month. Every month, you jot down when your period starts, how long it lasts, and how you feel.

Over time, you'll start to notice patterns. You'll see how many days your period usually lasts or what kinds of things happen right before it starts. This helps you get to know your body better and makes things much easier!

Knowing when your period will likely come means you can be prepared for it. You'll have all your period supplies ready, so you're not caught off guard. It also helps you know how you'll feel around the time of your period.

Most girls have a menstrual cycle that's about twenty-eight days long. What does that mean? It means that your cycle is the number of days from the first day of one period to the first day of your next period. But everyone's body is different, so your cycle might be shorter or longer. If it's between twenty-one to thirty-five days, that's okay too!

For example, if your period lasts five days and your cycle is about twenty-eight days, you can count twenty-eight days from the first day to get an idea of when your next period might start. Knowing this can help you be prepared with your period kit and ready for when the time arrives.

So, remember to keep track of the days and listen to how your body feels, and soon you'll be a pro at knowing when your period is coming.

Nowadays, some apps can help you track your cycle after you input your details. You need to input your period and cycle lengths, which will let you know when to expect your next period.

Some fun apps that will work for girls your age are Magicgirl Teen Period Tracker, Luna Period Tracker for teens, and Period Tracker Pinkllama, the Flo app, and My Period Calendar.

Managing Period Flow

I was excited to try out a pad for the first time. I had read all about it and was ready to become a pro. The pad came in a wrapper that made it look a bit like candy. So, I took it out and was prepared to go.

Pads have a sticky part on the back that keeps it in place inside your underwear. I carefully peeled off the paper covering the sticky part and was ready to attach it. But guess what? Instead of sticking it to the inside of my underwear, I accidentally stuck it right to my skin!

At first, I didn't notice anything unusual. I just thought, *This feels kind of funny, but maybe that's how it's supposed to be.* I walked around a bit, and the pad made this crinkly noise every time I moved. It was like I had a tiny pillow attached to my skin, making this funny rustling sound every time I took a step.

Soon, I felt the pad wasn't quite where it should be. I looked down and realized my mistake—I had put the sticky part on the wrong side! My pad was stuck to me like a sticky sticker, and it was uncomfortable.

Even though this was a bit of a mess at first, it was pretty funny. I laughed at my own mistake. It worked perfectly once I figured out how to put the pad on right! I wouldn't want you to make similar mistakes as mine, so I'll tell you how to change your pads and tampons.

To change your pad, first wash your hands with soap and water. Next, find a clean edge of the old pad and peel it off your underwear. If your pad has wings (the little flaps on the sides), start by pulling those off first. Grab the front or back edge of the pad and gently pull it away from your underwear. It should come off quickly.

Now, roll up the used pad with the messy side on the inside so it's all tucked away. Wrap it in some tissue paper if you have it, and then, throw it in the trash can. Never flush it down the toilet! Pads don't break down like toilet paper, so if you flush them, they can clog the pipes and make a big, messy problem.

Next, remove a new pad from its wrapper and peel off the paper strip on the back. Press the new pad, glue-side down, right in the middle of your underwear. Make sure it's centered and sticking well. And that's it! You're all set with a fresh new pad.

If you use tampons, you can change them this way: First, wash your hands with soap and water to keep everything clean. Then, find a quiet place where you can sit or stand comfortably.

To remove the old tampon, gently pull on the string hanging out of your body. If it feels a little sticky or hard to pull, don't worry—that's normal. Just keep pulling slowly and carefully until the tampon comes out. Once it's out, wrap it in tissue paper and put it in the trash. Don't flush tampons down the toilet; they can clog the pipes.

Now, let's get ready for a fresh tampon. Open the wrapper and read the instructions. Some tampons have an applicator that helps you place it inside, while others don't.

If it has an applicator, hold it by the end where the cotton part is. Gently insert the applicator into your body, using your fingers to push it in until it feels comfortable. Then, press the end of the applicator to push the tampon out and into place. After that, take out the applicator and throw it in the trash.

If the tampon doesn't have an applicator, you can use your fingers to gently insert it into your body. Make sure it's comfortable and not too high or low. If you feel any discomfort, it might not be in the right place, so try adjusting it a little.

Once the new tampon is in place, you're all set! Make sure you keep track of when you need to change it. Usually, you should change it every four to six hours or whenever it feels like it's getting full. And always remember to wash your hands after changing your tampon.

Dealing with Cramps

As I mentioned earlier, periods can bring many changes, one of which is stomach cramps. Stomach cramps aren't a big deal but because they linger for a while, they can become annoying.

Cramps are small pains or aches in your stomach. They feel like your stomach is pulling you from different sides. But don't worry; I have tips to help you deal with your period cramps. You can:

- **Use heating pads**

You can put a warm heating pad on your tummy or lower back. The heat can help make your cramps feel less uncomfortable. It's like a warm hug for your tummy! If you don't have a heating pad, a warm bath can help you relax.

- **Lie on your side**

Find a comfortable position. Try lying on your side with your knees pulled up toward your chest. This can help your sore back feel better. You can also put a pillow between your knees or lie on your back with a pillow under your knees.

- **Drink more water**

Sometimes, your tummy can feel sore because your body is holding extra water. Drinking lots of water – about six to eight glasses a day – enables you to feel better and can help your cramps feel less painful.

- **Take pain relievers**

I'm not a fan of taking pain relievers for period cramps, but they're not such a bad idea, either. A doctor should tell you which pain reliever would work best for you, but pop it in your mouth only when needed.

● Exercise

Light exercise, such as walking, can help you feel better. Moving around helps blood flow and can make cramps hurt less. Find something fun so it feels exciting to do!

● Avoid sugar

Eating too much sugar and caffeine can worsen cramps. Try a little dark chocolate or a cup of hibiscus tea if you want something sweet. It can help with those sweet cravings!

● See a doctor if the pain becomes unbearable

If your cramps are bad and nothing seems to help, talking to a doctor is a good idea. They can help you determine what's happening and find the best way to make you feel better.

Getting your period is a big step as you grow up, and it's normal to have questions about it. When you start to see small changes such as a little wet spot in your underwear or feel some tummy cramps, know that it's just part of this new phase. And if you're ever confused or something feels uncomfortable, it's okay to talk to someone.

The fun doesn't end with this chapter. There's more tea to spill in the next chapter, where we'll discuss your feelings and how to handle them during your period and puberty. Let's go to the next page!

Carly Gross

Chapter Four

Handling Your Feelings and Emotions

"If you retain nothing else, always remember the most important rule of beauty, which is: who cares?"
Tina Fey

Have you ever seen a swing in a playground constantly moving back and forth, up and down, with the help of nobody? That's how your feelings and emotions would look at this stage of your life.

Without warning, your emotions may shift from happy to sad, calm to angry, or excited to frustrated. You are feeling everything at once, and it's not a good feeling. These changes are too quick, and you don't like it.

Think of your hormones as water, and you are like an empty cup being overfilled with water. This is why the changes in your mood are so quick and feel strange to you. It takes a lot of getting used to, and thankfully, this chapter will guide you.

Puberty has its many ups and downs, and what you are experiencing is very much normal for your age. This chapter will discuss how you can handle these feelings and emotions like a champ.

Why Do I Feel This Way?

Your body is going through many changes, which are mostly influenced by an influx of hormones. These hormones are messengers that are important for the growth of your body.

The hormones that are responsible for how you feel are:

● **Estrogen**

This hormone is responsible for developing your sexual characteristics such as breasts. It's always fluctuating because it's just starting to be produced in your body, and your body needs time to adjust. This rise and fall in levels can influence your mood; it may cause sadness, irritability, or anxiety.

● **Progesterone**

This works together with estrogen, but it is more directly involved in regulating your menstrual cycle. The levels of this hormone are also not yet stable, and this can lead to mood swings.

● **Testosterone**

This is typically a male hormone, but it is present in females in small amounts. It's responsible for bone strength and growth spurts. Its instability may also affect your mood and cause you to be aggressive or moody.

● **Luteinizing Hormone (LH) and Follicle-Stimulating Hormone (FSH)**

These are produced by a gland in your brain called the pituitary gland, and they regulate the production of estrogen and progesterone. Their amounts also rise and fall and can affect your mood.

● **Cortisol**

This is called the stress hormone, and it also fluctuates. Low levels of cortisol may cause you to feel tired and sad. High cortisol levels may also cause you to feel anxious, nervous, and stressed. Cortisol fluctuations are often linked to stressful situations or hormonal changes in puberty.

In addition to these hormones, serotonin and dopamine are important neurotransmitters that regulate your mood. Neurotransmitters are chemicals that send signals to your brain.

Serotonin is known as the "feel-good" neurotransmitter. When it is balanced, it makes you feel happy and calm, but when it's low, that can cause you to feel sad and depressed.

Dopamine, the "reward" neurotransmitter, drives your motivation and makes you feel happy when you do rewarding things. It makes you feel pleased when you pass your examination, learn a new skill, or are praised.

When dopamine levels are high, this makes you feel motivated and focused. When they are low, that makes you feel tired, and you may experience difficulty concentrating. These two neurotransmitters are closely linked to the hormones produced during puberty, and they fluctuate just as your hormones do.

The feelings you are experiencing are normal, and they are there because your body is going through a natural process. Remember that everyone your age and older goes through these changes.

It's Okay to Be Upset

When the weather is stormy, it becomes gray and gloomy. Rain pours, everything gets wet, and you have to stay inside all day. The good part is that a storm doesn't last forever, and it's the same with your moods.

Your emotions are one of the ways your body communicates with you, and they help you understand yourself better, so be patient with the process.

You might feel sad, angry, and upset, or you might feel constantly tired and unmotivated. But all these feelings are normal, and it's okay to feel anything. Nothing is wrong with you in any way. Just as when there's stormy weather, you won't be upset forever.

I remember when I used to get upset at everything—at my sister, my mom, my friends, my pimples, my period. I was always angry. My mom made me understand that it's okay to feel all these emotions, and now I am here to tell you that it is okay to have all these feelings.

You are upset that you're confused. You want to know what's happening inside your body. You've probably asked yourself questions like:

Why do I feel this way? Why am I not normal? Why must I have a period? Why do I always feel sad? How do I stop being so angry? Why do I feel tired all the time? Why are my mood swings so intense? Why do I have so many worries? Why can't I stay positive? Why can't I control my emotions?

You have so many questions but no answers, and this upsets you. I understand you. Regardless of how you feel, know that you are normal and okay. You are great at who you are! You are special and unique! You're doing your best, and that's more than enough!

When you are upset, always remind yourself that you will feel better. It's only temporary, and it will pass. You also can develop coping strategies to make you feel better and help you reduce the questions in your head. Now, let's talk about those strategies.

Coping Strategies

These emotions are a lot to deal with, and you need a way to make yourself feel better and not become too overwhelmed.

The following strategies will help you cope with your emotions better. They are not perfect solutions, but they will help you feel more comfortable with yourself over time.

- **Talk it out**

You might feel overwhelmed and confused about how you are feeling, and the best thing you can do for yourself is to talk to someone. Talk to your mom, dad, close friend, teacher, or doctor.

Talk to whoever makes you feel comfortable, but I would advise talking to an adult. Adults know better because they have gone through puberty before.

• Put it on paper

Putting your feelings on paper helps make them less chaotic and more understandable, so grab a journal, notebook, or a piece of paper. When you've finished writing, you may choose to keep what you wrote or throw it out—it's up to you.

Remember, your writing doesn't have to be perfect, so don't fear writing down your thoughts. You also don't have to show anyone, but try to write down your feelings for yourself.

• Listen to music

You can put your headphones on and listen to songs that you love. It may be music that makes you happy, calm, silly, or groovy. It doesn't really matter. You can also listen to calming natural sounds like rain falling, a river flowing, or birds chirping; these are also great for relaxing and clearing your mind.

• Move your body

Exercise is known to improve the production of serotonin and dopamine, and these two are very important for regulating your mood.

You could go for a walk, dance to a groovy song, shoot some hoops, or just jump up and down. What matters is that you are moving your body.

Moving your body can also release stress and fill you with the energy needed to cope better. It's like magic for your mood.

● **Find your routine**

Having a routine is also great for relieving stress and not overthinking. You could write down a daily timetable for what to do before and after school and paste it into your room. Think of all your activities and try to make it a stable routine. This gives you rhythm and makes your moods more manageable because you are in control.

Also, your routine doesn't have to always go according to plan. Just make it a habit to have a rhythm every day.

● **Get some sleep**

You might be feeling upset because you are not getting enough sleep. The normal amount of sleep you are supposed to get is eight to ten hours daily. Maintaining this will help keep your mood balanced. Remove all distractions, try not to go to bed late, and aim to wake up well-rested and refreshed daily.

● **Comfort yourself**

If you have one, you can comfort yourself by cuddling your stuffed animal, pillow, or pet. You can also hug your mom, dad, siblings, or friends to make you feel comforted. This is a way to rely on something else to comfort you; it could be all you need to feel better.

● **Get creative**

You could make something creative. It could be drawing, writing, music, or craftwork. You can also join an art or dance class. This is a fun way to release your emotions without talking.

Get some paper, paints, crayons, or markers. You can draw, paint, or do some DIY creative craftwork. Let your imagination go as wild as you want, and have fun with it. Don't aim for perfection; instead, aim for creativity.

● Spot the triggers

Sometimes, your hormones are not the only issue; it could be something else. You should start paying attention to the things that set you off. It could be stress from school or home, friendship drama, or even lack of sleep.

Figuring it out means you'll be more in tune with your body, and that's great for you. It also makes you feel less upset with your body because you'll better understand what is happening to you.

● Watch what goes into your mouth

Junk food is nice, but too much of it can mess up your mood, and you don't want that. Try to be more healthy with your food by eating more vegetables and fruits, proteins, and healthy fats. Also, make sure to stay hydrated, and this means drinking plenty of water.

Doing these things will keep your energy up and make you feel more balanced in your emotions and feelings.

● Be kind to yourself

Your emotions are like a rollercoaster, and you may be angry at yourself for being unable to stop it. Don't let your emotions make you feel that way. Be kind to yourself and speak positively to your body.

Tell yourself that it's only for a short time and that you'll be okay. Don't speak harshly to yourself; instead, be nicer and more gentle with how you treat your body.

You are going through many changes, which is very normal. Use these coping strategies to manage your emotions better.

Remember, you got this!

Dealing with Stress

You are experiencing puberty, a rollercoaster of mood swings, and school is stressing you out. Everything seems to be hitting you at the same time. The good thing is, it's all very normal, and you can find ways to manage it.

You are feeling overwhelmed, but don't worry; there are ways to manage this stress. The following techniques can help you deal with stress and feel much better.

● **Breathing Exercises**
Breathing exercises reduce your heart rate, calm you down, and lower your stress level. They involve focusing on and controlling your breath, and you can do them anywhere and anytime.

To do this, find a quiet place. Close your eyes, and take a deep breath through your nose. Hold your breath for a few seconds, then slowly breathe out through your mouth. Do this five to ten times.

For box breathing, breathe in and count to four before holding it. Count to four as you hold your breath, then breathe out for four counts. Repeat it a few more times and feel your body calm down. You can do this when you know something stressful is coming up, such as a test or when you feel nervous.

● **Journaling**
A journal can be a private space where you write whatever you want without being judged by anyone. It's for you and your thoughts alone. Journaling can help you create a safe space for yourself.

Here are some fun ways to journal:

1. Choose a notebook or journal that you like. You can pick one with a cool design or decorate it yourself.

2. Write freely about how you truly feel. Be honest, and don't hide your thoughts from within your safe space.

3. You can write about things you are grateful for or happy about. You may also draw or doodle to make journaling more fun—it doesn't have to be serious.

4. Set a routine for your journaling time. It can be in the morning or right before you sleep.

5. You can also use prompts to write better. They could include, "What made me happy today?" "What are the things I like about myself?" "What do I want to achieve in life?" or "Why do I feel sad today?"

Have fun with journaling. Don't overthink what you write; it doesn't have to be perfect. Remember, it's just an outlet for your thoughts.

• Mindful Exercises

Mindfulness is the practice of focusing on the present. It helps you feel calmer and less worried, and it encourages a positive mindset. There are different ways to practice mindfulness.

Sit quietly and observe your environment. Pay attention to the sounds you hear, the smells entering your nose, and how your body feels on the chair you're sitting on. Breathe in and out, and be aware of how the air goes into your chest and leaves.

You can also take note of five things you can see, four things you can touch, three things you can hear, two things you can smell, and one thing you can taste. This is called the 5-4-3-2-1 grounding exercise.

Mindfulness helps your brain stay in the moment, reduce anxiety, be more aware of your environment, and not worry too much. You should make it a habit so you can benefit from it.

- **Positive Affirmations**

Make it a daily habit to speak positively to yourself every day. Here are some affirmations you can say to yourself:

1. *I am loved, and I deserve to be loved.*
2. *My mood swings do not define me.*
3. *I am strong, and I am capable of surviving anything.*
4. *I am unique and special.*
5. *I can achieve anything I set my mind to.*
6. *I am beautiful just the way I am.*
7. *Every day is a chance for me to smile and fly higher.*
8. *I believe in myself and my abilities.*
9. *I am proud of how far I have come.*
10. *I trust in the process of growing up, and I know I can do it.*

These affirmations are great for your mindset. You can say them to yourself in the morning before school or at night before you sleep. Do what makes you comfortable, and always say these words with conviction. I believe in you!

This chapter discussed handling your feelings and emotions, why you feel the way you do, and why you shouldn't be upset with yourself. We also covered strategies to help you deal with stress. The next chapter will focus on cultivating healthy habits. Let's go!

Chapter Five

Cultivating Healthy Habits

"A habit cannot be tossed out the window; it must be coaxed down the stairs a step at a time."
Mark Twain

If you have a garden full of beautiful flowers and you want to ensure that your flowers grow tall, what do you do? You give them water, let the sunshine in, and pull out the weeds, right? When you do that, the flowers should grow happy and strong.

Well, guess what? Your body is like that garden! Just as a garden needs water, sunshine, and grooming, your body needs a little love and care to stay healthy and happy.

As you grow older, your body will start to change! One of the significant changes is your menstrual cycle. This is something every girl goes through. But to feel your best during these changes, there are small things you can do every day. These small, good things are called healthy habits.

Healthy habits are all the little ways you can take care of yourself. They help you feel full of energy so you can play, learn, and do everything you love. Healthy habits aren't just for one part of your body, they help every part work together.

In this chapter, I will share some healthy habits you can start promoting. You'll learn how to take care of yourself in simple ways. And don't worry, it's not hard at all! These healthy habits will show your body some love, making you feel amazing!

Fueling Your Body

I remember when, as a young tween, I woke up to get ready for school one morning. Everything seemed pretty normal at first. But then, things started to feel a little weird. I noticed I was getting really irritated. My older sister was humming a song, and usually, I wouldn't care. But that morning, I snapped at her. She looked at me like I was being so mean, and honestly, I was. I didn't even know why I was so mad.

When I got to school, my best friend came over to me. I wasn't in the mood to speak at all. She talked about the movie we planned to watch that weekend, and I just shrugged. I could tell she was hurt, but I didn't know how to stop feeling this way.

Later, when I got home, I went straight to my room. As I looked in the mirror, I saw new pimples on my face. My mood was already off, and now my skin was breaking out. It felt like everything was going wrong all at once. Then, it hit me—my period was about to start. That explained a lot.

You see, when you're about to get your period, your body goes through all sorts of changes because of hormones. These changes can make you feel moody. You feel upset or irritated for no reason. And sometimes, they can even cause breakouts on your skin, like those pimples I was getting.

But here's the thing: My mood swings and pimples weren't just about my period. There was something else going on.

For the past few days, I had been eating a lot of junk food—chips, candy, soda, you name it. All the stuff that tastes good but isn't the best for my body. And I realized that what I was eating was making me feel worse!

When you eat a lot of sugary or oily foods, it can affect how you feel. For me, it made my mood swings even more intense, and it wasn't helping my skin either. So, after talking to my mom, I decided to make some changes.

I started eating more fruits and vegetables and drinking lots of water. I'd have a banana or carrots instead of reaching for a bag of chips. And guess what? It made a huge difference!

I noticed that I didn't feel as grumpy when I ate healthily. My mood swings weren't as bad, and I wasn't snapping at my sister or being rude to my friends. I felt calm and more like myself. And my skin? Well, it didn't clear up overnight, but over time, I had fewer breakouts.

Now, that doesn't mean I stopped eating my favorite snacks. I still have chips and candy sometimes. However, I try to balance that with the healthy stuff. I realized that eating well made me feel better—not just during my period but all the time.

So, what's the big lesson here? Well, when you're on your period or even just before it starts, pay attention to what you eat. Eating healthy foods gives your body the fuel to handle the changes.

Some foods give you energy. An example is whole grains; you can find whole grains in brown rice, oatmeal, or whole wheat bread. When you eat them, they help you feel full for a longer time, so you don't feel tired too quickly.

Fruits and veggies are also great! They're full of vitamins that make your body feel strong and fresh! Bananas help with cramps, and spinach adds iron to your body. Without enough iron, you will feel tired.

Protein is also important during your period. You can find protein in foods like eggs, chicken, nuts, and seeds. Protein helps your body repair muscles and enables you to regain lost blood faster.

And there's something basic but important. It's water! You might feel tired and weak if you don't drink enough water. So, make sure you drink plenty of water during the day. It helps your entire body stay strong during your period.

Now, when your period starts, your body might start asking for junk. You might have cravings for sugary or salty things. You'll always want something to munch on. This is totally normal!

Due to hormonal changes, your body starts to crave many things. I already talked about how bad junk food is for you. But the good news is you can enjoy some of your favorite comfort foods while staying healthy.

If you're craving something sweet, having a bowl of fruit salad can be just as satisfying as candy. However, if you don't want fruits, the next thing that comes to mind is chocolate, right? Instead of reaching for a big bar of candy, try dark chocolate.

Dark chocolate is a healthy type of chocolate. It has less sugar and is also packed with good nutrients. Dark chocolate tastes delicious and can satisfy your sweet tooth without giving you too much sugar.

Now, what about salty cravings? If you feel like eating chips or something crunchy, there are healthy ways to enjoy that crunch! You can try popcorn or baked chips. They will give you that salty flavor and satisfying crunch without being too heavy or oily.

You can also try nuts like almonds or cashews. They're full of healthy fats and can keep you satisfied for long.

Another great comfort food during your period is soup. Warm soups, such as chicken or vegetable soup, can be soothing. They're also packed with nutrients, especially if they're full of veggies.

If you're craving carbs, you can still healthily enjoy them. Whole-grain pasta or bread can satisfy your cravings. And they're more filling than regular white pasta or bread. You can add some veggies and lean protein, such as chicken or beans, to make it an even healthier meal.

I mentioned how vital water is earlier. But if you want something with more flavor, try herbal tea! It's warm and refreshing. And some teas, such as peppermint or chamomile, can help your cramps and bloating.

While you're on your period, your body is working hard, and it deserves a treat! Just remember to mix in some healthy choices so you can feel good.

Staying Active

Now that we've talked about all the yummy foods you can enjoy during your period, let's talk about something else that helps you feel good. It's staying active! I know it might sound strange, but moving your body, even just a little, can make a big difference when you're on your period.

You might wonder, *Why would I want to move around when I'm not feeling well?* It's totally understandable! When you have cramps, the last thing you want to do is exercise. But staying active can help your body feel better!

When you move around, your body releases some chemicals called endorphins. They're like happiness boosters that help you feel good. This makes you feel happy when you're on

your period. Being active also helps your blood flow better. This can make cramps less painful and help you feel more comfortable.

When I say "stay active," I don't mean you have to run a marathon or do anything too hard. Simple things such as walking, stretching, or dancing around your room can greatly help!

You can try out three activities: yoga, dancing, and light exercise. They're easy to do, and you can go at your own pace. You don't have to do much to feel better and can stop whenever you need to rest.

Let's start with yoga. Yoga is a way to stretch your body gently and breathe deeply. It helps you relax and feel more comfortable, especially with cramps. You can sit on the floor, take deep breaths, and start with simple stretches.

One stretch you can try is sitting with your legs crossed and reaching up toward the sky as if trying to touch the clouds! Another great one is lying on your back and hugging your knees to your chest. This can help make your tummy and back feel a lot better, especially when cramps come.

There's also a special yoga pose called a child's pose. For this, you kneel on the floor, stretch your arms out in front of you, and rest your forehead on the ground—like giving yourself a big hug. This move helps you feel calm and gives your body a gentle stretch without being too hard.

Next, let's talk about dancing! Who doesn't love to dance? Dancing is a fun way to move your body; the best part is that there are no rules. You can put on your favorite song, let loose, and dance however you want.

Dancing makes your blood flow better; this can make cramps feel less painful. The best thing about dancing is that it's fun. When you're having fun, you forget about feeling tired or achy.

You can also try light exercises. They're simple movements that don't take too much effort. One easy exercise is walking. You can walk outside or just take a short stroll around your house. Walking stretches your legs and gets your body moving.

Another easy exercise is doing leg lifts. To do this, you lie on your back, lift one leg at first, and then switch to the other leg. It's great for helping your body feel stronger.

Another light exercise you can try is arm circles. To do arm circles, stretch your arms out to the sides and make small circles with them. It's a fun way to stretch your arms and shoulders. You don't need to do them for long; just a few minutes can help loosen up your muscles and make you feel more comfortable.

All these activities are very easy to do and can help your body feel better during your period. So, the next time you're feeling a little low during your period, try doing one of these fun activities.

Rest and Recharge

Do you remember how I said that being active is good for you? Well, you should also know that getting rest is also essential. During your period, you'll need enough rest to function well. Let me tell you what happened to me as a tween.

One day, I had a big assignment due at school. I felt exhausted because my period had just started. I'd been working on my project all day, but I started feeling cramps, and I was becoming grumpy.

So, I decided to take a short walk around the block. It was a nice break, and the fresh air felt good. After my walk, I felt a little better, but I was still really tired.

I knew that rest is just as important as being active. So, I took a break from working on my project and put on my pajamas. I spent some time reading and relaxing, then went to bed early.

The next morning, I woke up feeling so much better! I had a whole night of sleep and felt stronger and ready to finish my project. I was glad I had taken the time to rest and care for myself.

I learned something important from that day. I realized that knowing when to rest and be active is important during your period. It's like balancing a see-saw. If you're too active or too tired, you'll feel uncomfortable. But if you balance things out, you'll feel much better!

When you're on your period, it's okay to take breaks and rest when you need to. Don't push yourself too hard if you're tired or have cramps. Resting helps your body heal and gives you a chance to relax.

And here's another important thing: good sleep! When you sleep well, your body can recharge and feel strong. It's just like plugging in a phone to boost the battery. That's what sleep does to you!

To get good sleep, try to have a bedtime routine. This means doing the same things every night before bed. You can decide to brush your teeth and read a book each night until your body gets used to it. This helps your body know when it's time to rest.

Also, make your room comfortable and quiet. Shut off all bright lights and loud sounds when you want to sleep. If you still find it hard to fall asleep, try reading a book or listening to some soft music before bed.

Hygiene Tips

Balancing rest, activity, and sleep is important during your period, but one more thing is important: having good hygiene.

When you have your period, your body will let out some blood. There'll be blood on your pads or tampons. And sometimes, you'll even get blood stains on your underwear. It's important to stay clean during this time so that germs don't start to grow and make you ill.

You also have to keep things clean to feel your best. Good hygiene helps prevent unpleasant odors and keeps you fresh throughout the day.

No matter what period product you use, changing it regularly is important. For pads, changing every four to six hours is a good rule of thumb. Tampons and menstrual cups should also be changed regularly by following the instructions on the package.

Now, let's talk about washing up. Always wash your hands before and after changing your period products. Keeping your hands clean helps prevent germs from spreading. When you wash your private area, use mild soap and warm water. Using strong soaps or douches can be too harsh on your sensitive skin.

Also, change your underwear frequently. It's always a good idea to wear clean, comfortable underwear during your period. You might even want to keep a few extra pairs if you need to change during the day. .

Carry a small bag with your period products and some extra underwear. That way, you'll always be prepared to handle any surprises your period brings. You'll also feel comfortable during your period.

This chapter has been a lot of fun, hasn't it? We've talked about so many cool things. But remember, it's not just about reading these tips, it's also about practicing them! The more you practice these tips, the more comfortable and happy you'll feel.

Keep having fun and caring for yourself, and you'll find joy every day of your period!

The next chapter is about everything self-care. Sounds fun already, right? Let's head over there!

Chapter Six

Practicing Self-Care

"Self-care is how you take your power back."
Lalah Delia

Self-care involves nurturing your body, mind, and soul. It's about doing the things that promote your happiness, health, and relaxation. It includes simple actions such as caring for your skin, getting adequate rest, exercising, and engaging in creative activities.

Self-care is a way of checking in with yourself and making sure you are taking care of your body's needs. As you experience puberty, practicing self-care becomes crucial.

This chapter will focus on helping you understand why you need your me-time. It has DIY ideas to pamper yourself and find creative outlets to relax and express yourself.

The Need for Me-Time

Self-care is about prioritizing your me-time. This means focusing on your physical, mental, and emotional well-being and making sure you feel good both inside and out.

So why is me-time important?

- **It boosts your confidence**
When you prioritize yourself, you recognize your self-worth, which boosts your confidence. You feel happy doing the things you love, and you become more positive about who you are.

- **It keeps you healthy**
Taking time for yourself allows your brain to relax, leading to improved focus when you return to school or other activities. It also reduces stress and promotes overall health.

- **It helps you feel better**

Focusing on yourself gives your mind and body a break, helping you relax and recharge after a busy day. It can be as simple as reading a book, listening to music, or participating in a sport you love.

- **It reduces stress**

Taking a break helps lower stress and makes it easier to handle tough situations. Think of it as pressing the "pause" button so you can come back stronger and more relaxed.

What can you do during me-time?

- Read a new book. Set a goal for each month by exploring a genre you're not familiar with or simply read one book a month.

- Start a book club with your friends, where you discuss your favorite books or read new ones together.

- Harness your creativity by drawing, coloring, or doodling. It's a great way to express yourself and relax. You could also join an art class if you want to learn more.

- Music is a powerful tool for unwinding and feeling better. Put on your favorite playlist and let the music help you relax.

- You can write in your journal. Reflect on your day, write down what you're grateful for, or capture any fun ideas you have. It's a great way to organize your thoughts.

- Sometimes, all you need to unwind is to watch your favorite show or movie.

- Learn a new dance by watching tutorials online or joining a dance class.

- Gather old pictures, stickers, or souvenirs to create scrapbooks. It's a fun way to preserve memories and tell your story.

- Pamper yourself by learning DIY methods to make a face mask, paint your nails, or enjoy a bubble bath.

It's not selfish to take time for yourself—it's necessary. When you feel good and relaxed, you can focus better and be more positive. It helps you become the best version of yourself. So, make time for yourself every day. It could be just a few minutes or an hour. It's all about you, so enjoy it.

DIY Pampering

I remember when my face started getting oilier than before, which led to breakouts. I had a lot of acne on my forehead and cheeks, which made me feel insecure about my appearance. I cried to my older sister, and she taught me ways to care for my skin and reduce acne. From that moment, I've grown, researched, and learned more, and I've been intentional about my skincare routine.

As your body undergoes changes during puberty, your skin changes too, so it's essential to know how to take care of it. You might notice your skin becoming oily or dry, or you might see a few pimples. Don't worry, it's normal!

During puberty, hormonal changes cause your skin to produce more oil, known as sebum, which can lead to breakouts. Sebum is meant to protect your skin, but too much of it can clog your pores, while too little can make your skin dry. Your skin might also start reacting to certain foods or products, so it's important to pay attention to how your skin behaves.

Additionally, your sweat glands become more active, especially in your underarm and pubic areas. This increases perspiration, and if not managed properly, it can lead to body odor.

By taking good care of your skin, you can manage these changes better. Here is a simple routine to help you care for your skin:

- **Wash your face daily**

This helps to get rid of the dirt, oil, and sweat that build up during the day, especially if you've been outside.

You can find a gentle face wash suited to your skin type. Gently massage the face wash into your skin for about a minute, then rinse and pat your face dry with a clean towel. Avoid washing too often to prevent drying out your skin. Twice a day is just perfect.

- **Use gentle products for your body**

Use a gentle soap or body wash to clean your body daily. Avoid using a harsh bathing sponge or washcloth, and focus on areas that are prone to sweat and odors.

Aim to bathe once a day, and if you engage in any physical activity such as sports or dancing, make sure to shower twice a day.

- **Moisturize after washing**

Choose a lightweight and non-comedogenic moisturizer for your body and face. Even if your skin feels oily, you still need a moisturizer. After washing your face, apply a small amount of moisturizer and gently rub it into your skin. Use it daily to keep your skin smooth and healthy.

- **Use deodorants or antiperspirants**

Deodorants are great for masking odor, while antiperspirants help reduce the amount of sweat, which in turn reduces odor. Choose the product you prefer based on your skin type. Apply it to clean, dry skin for the best results.

- **Drink plenty of water**

Water is the best thing for your skin. It keeps your skin hydrated, making it healthier. Aim for six to eight glasses of water every day, and drink more if you have been physically active.

- **Keep your hands away from your face**

Your hands pick up dirt and bacteria during the day, and when you touch your face, this can clog your pores and cause pimples. It's hard, I know, but you should try not to touch your face or pop your pimples, which can leave scars and make things worse.

- **Use sunscreen every day**

Sunscreen is important for your skincare. The sun's rays can damage your skin, causing sunburn and dark spots. So, sunscreen helps keep your skin protected and healthy. Use one that contains a physical blocker, such as zinc oxide, and has at least SPF 30. Apply it to your face, neck, and any part of your skin that is exposed. Remember to reapply it every couple of hours.

- **Keep your pillowcases clean**

When you sleep on your pillowcases all night, they can accumulate dirt and bacteria, which can worsen your acne. So, wash pillowcases regularly and make sure they are sun-dried before using them again.

- **Don't compare your skin to others**

Comparison is the thief of joy. Remember that everyone's skin is different—dry skin, oily skin, and acne-prone skin. It's essential to find what works well for you and stick to that routine. Don't steal your joy by constantly comparing yourself to others. Instead, focus on documenting your progress and celebrating your milestones.

Fun DIY Pampering Ideas

Skincare doesn't have to be boring or keep you stuck to a single routine. You can make it fun by creating fun DIY (Do It Yourself) ideas and enjoy the process.

Here are some DIY pampering ideas that are creative and enjoyable:

1. DIY Homemade Face Masks

Homemade face masks are skincare treatments made with ingredients you can easily find in your home. They help nourish, hydrate, or soothe your skin without requiring you to spend money on store-bought products. Here are some face masks you can try:

- **Honey and Oatmeal Face Mask**

  This mask is great for moisturizing your skin, especially if it feels dry and irritated. How do you make this?

  You'll need 1 tablespoon of honey, 2 tablespoons of oatmeal, and a little warm water. Mix the honey and oatmeal in a bowl, then add a little warm water to make a paste. Apply the mask to your face and leave it on for ten to fifteen minutes before rinsing off with warm water.

- **Avocado and Cucumber Mask**

  This mask is great for hydrating and nourishing your face. It is also great for reducing puffiness.

  What you need is ¼ avocado and 1 tablespoon of blended cucumber. Mash the avocado in a bowl and mix with the blended cucumber. Apply it to your face and leave it on for fifteen minutes before rinsing off.

- **Banana and Yogurt Face Mask**

  This mask is super-soothing and will give your skin a beautiful glow.

  You'll need ½ ripe banana, 1 tablespoon of honey, and 1 tablespoon of plain yogurt. Mash the banana in a bowl, add the yogurt and honey, and mix until it is smooth. Spread the mask on your face, let it sit for ten minutes, then rinse off with warm water.

2. Homemade Eye Pads

Eye pads are placed on the eyes to reduce puffiness, soothe the eyes, and possibly treat dark circles. Here are some DIY eye pads you can try out:

- Cut slim slices of cucumber and chill them in the fridge. Place them on your eyes and relax. This may reduce puffiness and hydrate the skin around your eyes.

- You can soak cotton pads in a small amount of rosewater in a bowl, then refrigerate for ten to fifteen minutes. Place them on your eyes for ten minutes. Rosewater has calming properties and can also reduce irritation.

- Melt some coconut oil and dip cotton pads in it. When well-coated, refrigerate for ten to fifteen minutes. Place them on your eyes for ten minutes. Coconut oil has moisturizing qualities and will soothe your eyes.

3. DIY Lip Balm or Scrub

Make a lip scrub with sugar and honey or coconut oil. Mix sugar with the honey or coconut oil to create a paste, gently massage this into your lips for a minute or two, then rinse off. You can add a few drops of your favorite essential oils.

This will moisturize and hydrate your lips and make them glow.

4. Nail Art Fun

You can set up a station in your room with nail polish in different colors. Add nail stickers and glitter to make it even more fun. You can try out fun designs alone, with your sister, or with a friend. You can also make a DIY cuticle oil by mixing a drop of lavender oil with a little olive or coconut oil, and massage it into your nails.

5. Bubble Bath or Foot Soak

Prepare a relaxing bubble bath with a few drops of essential oils such as lavender or chamomile. If a bath isn't possible, a warm foot soak with Epsom salts and a few drops of essential oil such as lavender or tea tree oil can also be soothing.

These ideas are not only fun but also help you develop a self-care routine that you can stick to. With these simple tips, your skin will stay healthy, and you will feel more confident.

Creative Outlets

Creative outlets are ways through which you can express your creativity and imagination. You can showcase your artistic talent and ideas through various creative activities.

Having a creative outlet has numerous benefits:

- It provides a space for self-expression. You can express your feelings and ideas without fear of judgment.

- Creating something unique can enhance your self-confidence and motivate you to do more.

- It's an outlet for the emotions you experience and serves as a means of coping in a healthy way.

- It stimulates your critical thinking, imagination, and problem-solving skills, which is great for cognitive development.

- Working in groups will improve your social skills, and you can make new friends by being a good group participant.

- Pursuing creative outlets can be a great way to relax and achieve mindfulness. It helps you unwind and take your mind away from stressful and negative thoughts.

Some common creative outlets include:

Drawing: This includes different mediums such as sketching, nature journaling, and doodling. For sketching, you can start by sketching your favorite flower, animal, or cartoon character. Use pencils, colored pencils, and markers to bring your ideas to life. For nature journaling, go outside and draw plants, leaves, or birds. It's a way to connect with nature and practice observation. For doodling, keep a small notebook to doodle in daily. Fill it with random drawings and patterns. Choose what you enjoy.

Creative Writing: This includes poetry, storytelling, or journaling. Storytelling includes writing short stories or creating a series about adventure or fantasy. Poetry involves writing simple poems and rhymes. Read poetry and write your own. It's a creative way to express your emotions and play with words. Journaling involves keeping a journal in which you write your thoughts, dreams, experiences, and affirmations.

Music and Dance: This includes learning an instrument, dancing, and singing. Pick up an instrument such as a keyboard, guitar, or cello and learn how to make music with it. Create dance routines to your favorite songs or learn steps from dance videos. Sing along to your favorite songs or write your own unique lyrics. It's a beautiful way to express your emotions.

Cooking and Baking: This includes trying easy recipes such as fruit salads, sandwiches with fun toppings, or fruit juices. You can also decorate cakes and cookies with colorful icings and sprinkles.

Start an Indoor Garden: Caring for a plant will teach you responsibility while providing fun at the same time. You can choose the type of plants you want and be dedicated to caring for them.

Don't overthink when you engage in creative outlets. Do what makes you happy, and don't compare yourself to others. Enjoy exploring your imaginative world and be proud of yourself as you learn how your creative mind works. Also, be patient with yourself.

And that's it for this chapter! I believe you've gotten many helpful tips on how to care for yourself and be more creative as a tween girl. The next chapter will focus on accepting and celebrating your unique body. You'll learn how to love your body and ways to deal with body image concerns.

Chapter Seven

Accepting and Celebrating Your Unique Body

"You are more powerful than you know; you are
beautiful just as you are."
Melissa Etheridge

One of the many changes you go through during puberty is your body changing. Being able to fully accept and embrace your body might seem like a lot to do. Know that your body is amazing, and these changes are normal. Every woman goes through it, and it's all part of the growing-up experience to become the beautiful woman you are meant to be.

You should never be ashamed of your body or try to hide it. It's your body, and you should embrace that.

Accepting and celebrating your body is also part of the experience. This chapter will show you how you can accept and nurture your amazing body.

Loving Your Body as It Grows

Your body is growing, and it's looking different from what you're used to.

Just a short time ago, you didn't have emerging breasts, growing hips, or acne. Now your body is transforming, and you don't recognize it anymore. It might feel strange, different, and even confusing. You might not even like these changes.

As you grow older, you have to learn to love your body, and here are some things to keep in mind:

• Embrace These Changes

You are growing into a beautiful young woman, and with that comes body changes. Your curves, newly growing hair, and pimples are signs of naturally progressing puberty. Take a moment to look at your mom, sister, or any girl around you, and observe how different they are from you. Doing this should help you understand that your changes are normal and you should embrace them. Your body is doing its work as it should.

• Don't Compare Yourself to Others

Your body changes might appear faster or slower than your friends, but that doesn't mean you are less of an adolescent than them. Your fingers not being equal is a reminder of how we are not the same, and everyone grows at their own unique pace.

• Be Nice to Your Body

It's not strange if you feel weird or embarrassed by your body changes but you need to be nicer to your body for being so good at what it does for you. Your body is preparing you for adulthood while still letting you run, dance, enjoy sports, and even laugh. Be nice to it.

• Confidence Comes from Within

Confidence starts when you think positively about yourself. Being confident is feeling happy with who you are, how you look, and what makes you feel good.

As your body is changing, remember that your body is strong, beautiful, and unique. Believe in yourself, knowing that you're amazing!

- **It's Okay to Ask Questions**

Puberty can be confusing, and talking to an adult or a friend is great. Don't be too shy to ask why you feel a certain way or look a certain way. Share all your concerns with a trusted person, and this will build your confidence.

As long as you are trying to understand your body better, don't be scared to ask questions. There is no such thing as a silly question.

- **Everyone's Body Is Unique**

Take a look around you and see if everyone looks the same. You'll find that nobody looks the same way. This shows that our bodies are unique, yours included. We are different in height, shape, hair texture, and even size. You are you, and that's called being unique.

Self-Love Is Key

Embracing yourself also means that you practice self-love. Self-love means that you care for and accept your body the way it is. You treat your body nicely and are confident in it.

So how do you practice self-love?

- **Take Care of Your Body**

Be nice to your body by practicing good hygiene, eating healthily, hydrating yourself, and getting enough sleep. You should also speak positively to your body every day.

- **Do What You Love**

Engage in fun activities like dancing, riding a bike, reading, or drawing. Do things that you love, and be happy about yourself. Spend time with yourself and enjoy every moment.

- **Be Grateful**

Write a list of things you are thankful for, such as your body, your family, or something good that happened to you recently. This will help you stay positive and happy.

- **Write a Letter to Yourself**

This is a kind way to appreciate yourself better. In the letter, write the things that make you happy. Talk about your dreams, goals, and whatever makes you feel good. It doesn't have to be perfect. Keep it safe, and read it when you feel down.

- **Spend Time with Your Loved Ones**

Spend time with the people who make you feel loved, like your family or friends. Avoid negative people.

Your body is doing what it should do, and that's so great. You should be proud of it. Remember to always treat your body with care, respect, and love. Don't forget that it's not just you going through puberty, but you are still special regardless.

What Makes You Special?

You are special, strong, and beautiful. Your strengths, interests, and attributes are what make you who you are, and even though your body is changing so fast, you are still amazing.

If you ever notice you're being overly critical of yourself, remind yourself of the strength you possess and how special you are. These are some of the things that make you special.

- **Your Unique Personality**

You might be kind, creative, determined, or patient. Regardless of what type of personality you have, that is one of the unique things about you. Your personality makes other people like you, and that's cool.

- **Your Talents and Hobbies**

What are the things you love to do that make you happy? It could be drawing, playing an instrument, singing, writing, solving math, or playing sports. Your talents and hobbies are your passion, so celebrate whatever you are passionate about. They make you unique.

- **Your Kindness and Empathy**

You might be the type of person who listens to her friends, cares about others, or helps them when they feel sad. These are all attributes that make you special.

- **Your Dreams and Goals**

Everything about you is special. Your dreams and goals show what you love, what you are about, and what matters to you.

- **Your Strengths**

Puberty means that your body is developing. This is also a sign of strength.

Your body can do many beautiful things. You are becoming a young woman whose body is capable of doing amazing things, and that's impressive.

Dealing with Body Image Concerns

Imagine if you had to eat just one type of food every day even though there were other varieties available. How would that make you feel? Or what if someone told you that there is only one way to walk, and regardless of where you come from, you have to walk that way, forgetting the fact that legs are different and people don't all walk the same?

Here's the thing—the body standards in our society today work in a similar way. According to unrealistic standards, every woman must look, eat, walk, and talk a certain way, forgetting that we're unique and different.

As you grow and experience puberty, it's normal for you to have concerns about your body. It's even worse when all you can see around you are images of "perfect" bodies that don't look like you at all. These images are called body standards.

The media paints an unrealistic picture. TV shows, movies, magazines, and social media are some of the tools used to advertise these "perfect" bodies. These pictures are heavily edited and filtered. Even the models in these images don't look perfect when you meet them. They spend hours on each picture, making sure all the "imperfections" are carefully removed. These pictures are not real, and they are designed to make you feel bad about your body so they can sell you their products.

Bodies come in all shapes and sizes, and we can't all look alike. Your skin color may look like someone else's, your hair may be similar, or your height may be the same. But despite the similarities, there are also many differences.

There is really no right way to look. Fashion and trends will definitely change, but your unique body remains yours. These standards are the reasons why you need to stay true to yourself and embrace and appreciate yourself. Understand why these standards exist and choose not to give in to the marketing trends.

What should matter to you is having a good personality, being respectful to your body, and being kind to others and yourself.

Society often pushes unrealistic ideals that lead to unhealthy comparisons. The truth is, beauty comes in different shapes and sizes, and you don't need to look a certain way to be worthy or healthy. With so much information online, it's difficult to know what's right and wrong. So, let's clear up some misconceptions about body image. This is to help you understand your body better and feel more confident.

Myth 1: There is only one way to be beautiful.

Beauty is not one-size-fits-all. It comes in many forms. There is no right size, normal color, or perfect shape. It's normal to have a body that is not like those in the magazine. Be confident and proud of your body.

Myth 2: You have to look like models and celebrities.

Not only are their images edited and filtered, but they also have teams of makeup artists, professional photographers, and trainers who carefully create their images. It's unrealistic and not what anyone should aspire to.

Myth 3: Your worth is defined by your appearance.

This is not true at all. Your worth is defined by who you are on the inside. It's your talent, your personality, your actions, and your kindness to others. Your look is only a tiny part of what defines you.

Myth 4: You need to constantly diet to maintain a "perfect" body.

Constant dieting or taking it to the extreme is harmful to your body and your self-esteem, and it's not necessary for having a healthy body. Instead, develop a healthy relationship with food and listen to your body.

Myth 5: Changing your body will solve all your body insecurities.

This is not true at all. Changing your body only means you give in to unrealistic body standards, and your problem will only get worse. What you need to work on is your self-esteem and self-love.

Myth 6: Body positivity means loving how you look.

Body positivity is about accepting, embracing, and respecting your body. You should love your body even when you don't feel so good about how you look. It's all about understanding and recognizing your self-worth and being kind to yourself.

Finally, believing these myths can make you feel insecure about your body. Choosing not to believe them will improve your confidence and self-love. You don't need to change who you are to fit a standard. Be your own standard.

In the next chapter, we'll discuss building your safe space, how to be comfortable talking about your period, and how to start conversations about your period. You'll get helpful tips on how to have a support system.

Chapter Eight
Building Your Safe Space

"Sometimes self-care is creating a safe space within yourself where you can exist fully, where your feelings can have their own sanctuary."
Alex Elle

The puberty stage can feel overwhelming, confusing, and strange. You may even feel a little lost because of these new changes that you have to experience. It's normal to feel all these emotions, but there are things you can do to make yourself feel better. One of them is to create a safe space for yourself.

A safe space is a place that makes you feel calm, happy, and relaxed. It could be in your surroundings or within yourself. You have to be comfortable and free to be yourself in this space.

What are the things that make you feel calm and happy? What are the things that make you smile?

It could be a corner in your room with everything you love, such as your favorite books. It could be drawing what makes you happy or sitting under a tree to listen to birds and feel the wind on your skin.

Think about these things as you aim to build your safe space. Creating your safe space is not just about finding a physical space; it's about finding it within yourself and owning it.

This chapter will focus on how you can create your own safe space, talk about your period, and build your support system.

Creating Comfort

When I had my first period, my mom talked to me about what was happening to me. She also talked about period sanctuaries and why I needed them. She showed me pictures of her period sanctuary when she was young, and I immediately wanted my own.

You might be wondering, *what are period sanctuaries?*

Period sanctuaries are warm, cozy spaces that are personal to you and provide comfort during your menstruation. The idea is to create a soothing environment where you can take care of yourself and rest.

For me, I chose a spot by my window, gathered my favorite soft pillows, and curled up with my blanket and my teddy bear. Sometimes, I'd read a book, sleep, or play some soothing music. I also stocked my sanctuary with pads, snacks, and a bottle that I'd filled with warm water. I chose

the spot because it had a beautiful view of our garden, and I loved seeing the beautiful flowers.

The sanctuary helped me reduce my stress, feel safe and calm, and focus on myself. It made me more in tune with myself and reduced the negative thoughts in my head.

Building your period sanctuary is fun and feels special. So if you want to build one, here are some ideas to help you set it up:

- **Find your spot**

You can choose your bed, a corner in your room, a quiet place in your house, your favorite chair, or even a space in your closet. Make sure it's a place where you feel comfortable and can always return to when you need a break.

- **Add your soft essentials**

Gather your soft pillows and your fluffy blankets. You can also add your favorite stuffed animals or a plushie. These would make your space warm and inviting.

- **Add your favorite things**

These may include your stuffed animals, favorite books, or a lamp with gentle lighting. It can also be art supplies for drawing and painting or a journal to document how you feel.

- **Bring your essentials**

Stock your space with the essentials you need during your period, such as your pads or tampons, water bottles, heating pads, wipes and tissues, and snacks. You can put all of these in a box or a basket.

- **Make it entertaining**

These might include art supplies or calming music. You can create a playlist or ask someone to help you with it. All these should bring you joy and keep your mind off the discomfort.

- **Add some extra personal touches**

You can decorate your space with photos, drawings, or artwork that makes you feel happy. You can also add your favorite scents. This might be in the form of scented candles, a sachet of dried flowers, or a diffuser. You can also add lighting that you like.

All these touches make your space feel more personal and special to you.

Now that you know what to do to create a period sanctuary, you can start building yours. It's your world, and you can make it whatever you want it to be.

Talking About Your Period

"Mom? Dad? I need to talk to you" sounds very simple yet feels very daunting. Despite being prepped by my mom, I still found it difficult to open up when I had my first period, and I experienced a rollercoaster of mood swings. It wasn't until my sister noticed I wasn't coping well that she called it to my mom's attention.

Don't be like me. Be willing to talk to someone about the things that are confusing you. You have never gone through this experience before, so you need a better understanding, and you can't get that without opening up.

Starting a conversation about what you are feeling and knowing the right people to talk to might feel difficult, but it doesn't have to be. There are people you can talk to for guidance and support.

Experience is the best teacher. When choosing who to talk to, ensure it's someone who has gone through what you are going through and understands what you are saying. Their experience would be a more helpful guide on how to navigate your new stage. The following are people you can share your experience with:

- **A Parent or Guardian**

Opening up to your parents might seem difficult, but trust me, they are the best people you can talk to. They have gone through puberty, and they know how it feels. They can provide you with the supplies, support, and information you need about your period.

My mom was the most resourceful person around me, and I'm so happy I spoke to her back then. Because of her support, I was able to successfully navigate my period and all that comes with it.

- **A Close Family Member**

You can talk to an older sister, aunt, grandmother, or female cousin. They have all gone through similar experiences and can share them with you. You might even feel more comfortable talking to them.

- **A Trusted Teacher or School Nurse**

You might have a teacher that you like and trust, or you could confide in the school nurse. They can offer you valuable advice and make sure you feel safe and comfortable enough to talk about your period.

- **A Close Friend**

Despite being as young as you, a friend can be very helpful to talk to, especially one who has had her period.

I was in class when I had my first period, and my friend was the one who helped me through it that day. She supported me and made sure I felt normal. She was able to do this because she had started her period earlier than I did, and she knew things I didn't know.

- **A Coach or Mentor**

If you feel embarrassed about telling anyone else, you might have a coach or mentor you trust. Be careful, though, and make sure it's someone with a good track record.

When choosing whom to tell, ensure it's someone you are comfortable with and trust; someone who is supportive and respects your feelings. Choose someone patient, kind, and a good listener. You need someone who will hear you out and also take you seriously; someone who will not judge you but give you great advice.

Finally, remember that it's your choice. Talk when you want to, and don't feel pressured to share with anyone you're not comfortable with or to share things you don't want to. Take your time and open up when you are ready to do so.

How to Start Conversations About Your Period

The first thing to do is to let someone know what you need. "I need to talk to you" is a simple way to start a conversation.

You can follow up with simple questions and statements like:

- *Can I ask you something about periods?*
- *I have a question about my body.*
- *I've been feeling nervous about my period.*
- *I think my period might be starting soon.*
- *How did you handle things when you were my age?*
- *I don't like feeling so emotional during my period.*
- *Why does my stomach hurt so much?*
- *Do I need to do anything special for my period?*
- *My periods have been irregular. What do I do?*
- *Is it normal to have acne during periods?*

These questions open the door for your parents to come in and answer your questions. This way, they can reassure you while understanding exactly what you need.

Listen to them when they talk. Ask them about their day and listen to them talk about it before you jump in with your questions. Additionally, pay attention as they answer your questions, and ask more questions when you feel confused or lost.

When starting conversations about your period, pay attention to the following:

- **Be prepared**

Think about what you want to say beforehand. You could write your questions down so you can ask them more effectively. This makes it easier for whoever you choose to talk to and helps them understand exactly where you are coming from.

- **Don't be ashamed of asking questions**

Periods are normal, so don't feel ashamed for asking questions you don't understand. The person you chose was once confused like you, and they also asked someone questions. But look at them now—they've grown to become knowledgeable!

- **Don't expect perfection**

Remember that the person you're talking to doesn't know everything, so don't be disappointed if they can't answer all your questions. What matters is that they listen to you and care about you.

- **Show gratitude**

Let the person you choose know that you appreciate them listening and talking to you. You should say, "Thank you" or "I'm glad that we talked." This will also make them more willing to talk to you the next time you need them.

Your Support System

A support system is a group of people who are willing to talk, listen, and back you up at all times. Your support system doesn't have to be your family; it could be your friends or even trusted strangers. They are your people.

Your support system offers advice, answers your questions, and helps you feel safe and confident in yourself. The main focus of your support system is growth.

Talking about your period with your support system helps you feel less alone and more aware of what is happening to your body. Your support system should include mostly people who have experienced periods and can support you better.

So, what's the importance of having "your own people?"

• For Encouragement

Every day won't be all blue, but there'll be bad days. You need your people on such days to be your support and encourage you.

When I started my period, I didn't understand anything about it. With encouragement from my mom, sister, and friend, I was able to navigate it better. If they hadn't encouraged me, I wouldn't have been able to understand what was happening or feel confident about it.

You might get so engrossed in your daily activities that you forget to look after yourself. It happens to the best of us, and it's natural.

Your support group is there to help you. They can assist with getting snacks, regulating your sleep schedule, and recommending products when you experience breakouts.

• For Better Recovery

Life is filled with ups and downs, and having a support group beside you can help during the sad times. Sad times might push you to isolate yourself or drown in loneliness, but with your people around, you'll feel less sad.

Your support system can also help you during cramps, mood swings, and when you are stressed. They can help you recover.

Knowing When to Ask for Help

Having a support system is great, but you also have to know when to ask for help. These are times when it might be good to ask for help:

• When you are worried and scared

You might be experiencing mood swings, heavy periods, or cramps and be feeling worried or scared about what's happening. It's important to talk to someone who can help you feel better and give you a better understanding of your situation.

- **When you have questions**

Every time you have a question about your period, your body, or puberty, you should ask someone you are comfortable with and trust.

- **When you are in pain or discomfort**

When you have cramps or headaches, or you feel uncomfortable about something going on within you, ask for advice. Don't keep it to yourself.

- **When you don't feel ready**

One thing about puberty and periods is that you are never ready, which is why it's important to talk to someone. Your period might start suddenly, or you might notice changes in your body and feel confused. Talk to someone.

- **When you feel embarrassed or unsure**

Feeling shy, embarrassed, or uncertain is a normal reaction to your body's changes. Sharing your feelings can help you feel more comfortable and confident.

- **When you need supplies**

When you're new to starting your period, it might begin suddenly and in places where you don't have supplies. Having a support system means you can reach out to them, and they will provide you with what you need.

- **When you feel sad and alone**

Talking to someone when you feel sad or alone can make you feel better, which is why having a support network is important. They will remind you that you're not alone.

It's okay to talk about your feelings and seek the support

you need without fear of judgment. Your support people are there to comfort you and be your safe space.

- **When you want to learn more**

You might want to know more about puberty, periods, mood swings, and personal hygiene or receive advice about how to better your life. Your support system can also provide you with valuable insight into your future and what you want to do as you grow up. This is why it's so important.

Seeking Help from Your Support System

Talking to your support system might feel weird and awkward at first, but it gets better when you are confident and feel sustained by them. So, here are ways to encourage the conversation and make it easier:

- **Start small**

Don't jump into everything you want to know in the first discussion. Start with simple topics, ask about their experiences, or share how you feel. You don't have to bring up everything at once.

- **Choose the right moment and environment**

You should not start your conversation when you know they are busy or worried. Pick a quiet time when they are relaxed and in the right state to focus on you. You should also pick a private place such as your room, their office, or during a walk to start the conversation.

- **Be honest about your feelings**

It's okay to be nervous even though fully able to say what's on your mind, but regardless, try to be honest. Don't exaggerate or downplay your feelings; let your group understand exactly what you need. This aids them in helping and supporting you.

- **Ask questions to understand better**

Ask questions such as, "What was it like for you?" or "What more should I expect?" These are great follow-up questions that are very helpful during a conversation.

- **Use "I" statements**

Personalize your experience so the person you are talking to takes you seriously. Say things like "I'm feeling confused," "I don't understand what is happening," or "I feel sad and I don't know why" to express yourself clearly.

- **Stay Calm and Positive**

Be relaxed and calm as the conversation begins. Remind yourself that these conversations are important for your growth and understanding.

You are not alone—remember that.

Many girls your age are experiencing the same changes as you are, and even though it feels like nobody understands what you are going through, many people do.

Getting your period is a normal part of growing up, and there are many people who wish to support you. Don't be hesitant to speak up and ask for what you need.

This is your body, and you deserve to feel confident and supported. You have people around you who are willing to help—your family, friends, teachers, and other trusted adults. They have gone through it, understand it, and are willing to listen and answer your questions.

In the next chapter, we'll discuss how to build your confidence, prepare for the future, empower yourself, and share your knowledge with others. We'll also discuss the importance of speaking positively to yourself. You are doing so well, and I'm so proud of you.

Carly Gross

Chapter Nine
Growing Up with Confidence

"Nothing can dim the light that shines from within."
Maya Angelou

When I experienced puberty, I was hard on myself. I was far from being confident, didn't like who I was, and always shrank in shame instead of raising my head high. I was too critical of my body and didn't give myself the grace to experience puberty in a healthy way. I dimmed my light with my negative thoughts and didn't enjoy the wonderful experience.

I'm sure you can already tell that I regret the way I acted toward myself. Yes, I do! I should've been more confident. Well, I believe you'll do better. Don't be like my old self.

Confidence means trusting and feeling good about yourself. It means that you know you can handle challenges and be triumphant. Building your confidence is a lot of work, but it's the best thing you can do for yourself at this stage of your life. Tweens with a high level of confidence understand their worth and are willing to do what it takes to be better.

The results will not come if you don't put in the work, and this chapter will show you how to make the effort to be more confident and positive.

What's Next?

Puberty is like going on a journey. On that journey, you should expect different things to come your way. Your body and mind will change, and you will always discover new things about yourself. These changes can be overwhelming, nerve-wracking, or exciting, but you have to be prepared for what's to come.

How do you get ready for what is ahead of you?

- **Stay Informed**

Kofi Annan once said, "Knowledge is power. Information is liberating." This means that being informed will empower you to handle changes more successfully than if you didn't welcome learning.

Puberty is part of growing up, and learning about it will keep you informed, comfortable, and more confident. You can stay informed by reading books, talking to trusted adults, or watching videos about puberty.

Asking questions is also a way to stay informed and ready. Whether it's about your menstrual cycle, body changes, mood swings, or skincare, make sure to ask. Your questions are not silly. See them as an opportunity for you to learn and feel more at ease with your body and mind.

- **Know Your Body**

Your body is your friend, so get to know it. This involves paying attention to your body—how it feels and how to take care of it. For example, understand how your menstrual cycle works. You can keep track of the number of days, your premenstrual symptoms (PMS), or even the types of feminine hygiene products your body likes and dislikes. You can also take time to learn about your hygiene, nutrition, and sleep cycle.

Be observant, and don't shy away from asking questions when you notice differences in patterns. Your observations might just save you from something that shouldn't have happened to you.

● Embrace changes

The only constant thing in life is change, and change is a big part of puberty. It might feel uncomfortable on most days, but remember that it's part of the process of growing up.

Your body will continue to grow, so embrace all these changes and see your body as your friend. You would want your friend to grow, right? Focus on the positives such as becoming smarter, bigger, and stronger. You are evolving into a better version of yourself, and that's something worth celebrating.

● Prepare for milestones

Some of the milestones you will go through are getting your period, buying your first bra, meeting new friends, and even getting taller. There are so many amazing things ahead of you.

Every milestone is an opportunity for growth, self-discovery, and becoming even more amazing. A good way to prepare for your milestones is to stay informed. When you know what might happen, you are not caught off guard. You already know how you will handle problems before they happen. You might carry period supplies before your first period and practice good hygiene. Another way to prepare is by talking to someone about what to expect.

● Take care of your mental health

Mental health refers to the wellness of the mind. When you are mentally healthy, you are at peace with yourself and others. As your body changes, your emotions change too.

Finding ways to deal with these emotions in a healthy way is essential for your growth. This includes sleeping well, eating healthily, being physically active, spending time with family and friends, and practicing mindfulness.

Your mind is powerful, and it's important to take care of it as you navigate through puberty. Remember to prioritize both your physical and mental well-being during this time. Remember to stay curious, keep learning, and trust yourself as you grow up.

Empowering Yourself with Confidence

Puberty is a time when your body and mind undergo changes. It's normal, and during this process, you might lose confidence in yourself or feel overwhelmed. However, building your confidence is crucial at this stage.

Here are some reasons why you should build your confidence:

- **It makes you feel happier**
When you like yourself and feel more confident, you are happier and more comfortable. You are less worried and nervous about how you look or feel. You understand why you go through puberty and focus on the positives.

You celebrate your uniqueness instead of constantly berating yourself and speaking badly about yourself. You laugh more and celebrate life more.

- **You believe in yourself**
When you feel more confident, you know you can do anything you set your mind to. You don't restrict yourself;

rather, you spread your wings and fly high like an eagle. You stay true to yourself and are more positive about who you are.

● **You make better decisions**

Building confidence in yourself helps you trust your ability to make positive choices that impact your life, whether they're related to friends, family, school, or life in general. You are capable of putting yourself on the right path. It also means you are willing to learn and understand things before jumping into them. You not only make decisions, but you also care about the consequences.

● **You handle challenges better**

Confidence helps you face challenges better without fear. Even when something goes wrong, you don't panic or become overly critical of yourself. Instead, you observe, learn from your mistakes, and try again. You understand that challenges are an opportunity to grow and should not make you feel bad about yourself.

● **You can speak up for yourself**

When you are confident, you don't back down or cower in fear when you know you are right. You stand up for yourself and say what you think without being rude or arrogant. It also helps you stand up to bullies who will feed off your low self-confidence to treat you badly.

High self-confidence means their words don't affect you because you have built yourself up to know you are not less than you really are.

● **You become open to trying new things**

Confidence makes it easier for you to be adventurous and curious about your environment. You can try on a new skirt or dress without feeling insecure about how it fits, or you can try a new hobby without fear of failing, whether it's cheerleading or basketball or a new skill. You are open-minded and willing to make yourself better.

● **You get along with others**

When you get along with yourself better, you can get along with others without fear of judgment. Confidence means that you won't feel jealous or compare yourself to your friends. Instead, you compliment them—let them know what is unique about them and how much you appreciate them in your life.

• You aim to reach your goals

When you are confident in your abilities, you are not scared to dream. You work hard and keep moving until you reach your goals. Failure doesn't stop you from trying over and over again until you get it right.

Empowering yourself involves building your confidence, developing a positive mindset toward life and yourself, and acquiring skills that will help you navigate puberty effectively. It's believing in yourself by learning and taking the steps needed to do so.

Here are some ways to boost your confidence:

• Use daily affirmations

Daily affirmations are short positive sentences that you say to remind yourself of how great you are and to build your confidence. When you say these affirmations daily, you start to believe them, and that belief is essential for boosting your confidence.

Remember the positive affirmations I shared earlier? Now is the time to learn how to use them effectively. You can also create a personalized list of positive things you'd like to say to yourself daily.

You can repeat these affirmations when you want to. It can be in the morning before going to school or at night before bed. Find what makes you feel comfortable and focus on truly believing them as you say them.

Just saying them might be boring, so here are fun and creative ways to incorporate affirmations into your day:

• Mirror Motivation

You can stand in front of your mirror and say two to five affirmations to yourself. Repeat them out loud while staring at yourself. You can be dramatic while saying it too. It's all up to you.

- **Positive Sticky Notes**

Write your affirmations on colorful sticky notes and place them around your room in different spots. They can be on your desk, in the pockets of your shirts, on the mirror, or on the door.

- **Affirmation Cards**

You can create a deck of cards or ask someone to help you with this. Pick a card each day and focus on that affirmation. You can carry it to school or wherever you go that day.

- **Bedtime Rituals**

Every night, before you go to sleep, say a few affirmations to yourself. This helps you end the day with the positivity, calmness, and confidence needed for the next day.

- **Affirmation Art**

You can create posters with colorful markers and pens, writing down your favorite affirmations. These can be hung in your room as a visual reminder of your positivity.

These methods make your affirmations more personal, creative, and engaging. With constant practice, you will help build your self-esteem over time. These affirmations will help you feel more confident and ready for the day.

- **Be kind to yourself**

Yes, you are making mistakes, but no, you should not be hard on yourself. Say to yourself, *It's okay to make mistakes, and I will learn from them*. This is you being patient and kind to yourself even when things are not going the way you planned.

Being kind to yourself means treating yourself with care, acceptance, and understanding—when things are perfect and when they aren't. It's telling yourself, *I'll do my best* instead of *I can't do this*. It's giving yourself enough grace to try things, make mistakes, learn, and try again. These are some ways to be kind to yourself:

- **Embrace your uniqueness**

A great way to show kindness to yourself is by accepting that everyone is different, and that's what makes you unique. Don't compare yourself to others or think that you are inferior to other people. Understand that everyone has their own strengths and weaknesses.

- **Do what makes you happy**

Take your time to do the things that make you happy, whether it is drawing, reading, starting a new skill, or playing with your friends. Also, take breaks when you feel tired and overwhelmed. Don't be afraid to ask for help; know when to reach out to others for support.

- **Challenge negative thoughts**

Whenever a negative thought comes to your mind, challenge it. Ask yourself why you are feeling that way and what you can do to make it better. Be intentional about avoiding negativity toward yourself.

- **Be your own friend**

Talk to yourself like a friend. Use the same comforting and motivating language that you would use with a friend who is upset or being hard on themselves. Remind yourself that it's okay and that you will be fine.

Being kind to yourself is not easy, but with consistent practice, it can become part of your life. Constantly remind yourself that you are worthy of kindness, love, and happiness. You are worth it!

- **Surround yourself with positivity**

What you allow around you can influence how you feel and behave toward yourself. So, make sure to constantly surround yourself with positivity whether it's through inspirational books, music, friends, or hobbies that reinforce a healthy mindset.

Engage in enjoyable activities with your friends and family. Laugh and cherish your time with them. Being around positive influences will make you happier, more confident, and more resilient.

- **Set realistic and achievable goals**

One of the reasons you are being hard on yourself is that you are setting unrealistic goals for yourself and failing to achieve them. You tend to lack confidence in yourself when you fail. You need to set achievable goals. Here are ways to set realistic and achievable goals:

- **Start small**

  Starting with simple and small goals is important if you want to achieve them. For example, you can practice math for twenty minutes a day instead of wanting to be the best at math. The practice is designed to help you gradually improve at math and ultimately become the best at it. Starting small helps you build your confidence and demonstrate that it's achievable.

- **Be specific with your goals**

  Instead of saying, *I want to be healthier,* be more precise, such as saying, *I will eat more vegetables every day.* This is specific to being healthy, and it is realistic.

- **Set a time frame**

  Time frames make your goals more achievable. For example, say, *I will drink more water every day* or *I will read a book every month.* It's a clear target, and you don't feel rushed to do it.

- **Celebrate your progress**
  No matter how small your success seems to you, reward yourself for it. It might be finishing a chapter of a book or solving a math equation. Your reward doesn't have to be grand; let it be something that makes you happy and proud of yourself.

- **Make it personal**
  Make your goals something you truly want, not something you're pressured to do. If you're passionate about learning an instrument or improving your art, pursue it. Don't join that book club just because it is cool to do so—do it because you want to read more books and improve your vocabulary. Or better still, join a club that suits your goals.

  When your goals are more personal, you're more motivated to achieve them.

- **Ask for help when you need it**
  You might get stuck on your goals or need advice on how to approach them, so ask for help. Whether it's from a parent, sibling, or friend, getting support is part of achieving any goal in life.

- **Track your progress**
  You can track your progress with a journal, calendar, or goal chart. You'll be more motivated to keep working when you can see your progress.

- **Reflect on the results**
  Once you achieve your goals, reflect on how your results make you feel. Are you proud of them? Did you learn something? Do you want to set a new goal? This reflection will help you understand yourself better and apply what you learned to future goals.

Sharing Your Knowledge

Now that you know so much about puberty, what to expect, and how to deal with everything that comes with it, you might meet younger girls who need help, so knowing what to do is important. Sharing your knowledge can make young girls such as you feel empowered. Here's how you can do it:

- Improve your listening skills. This way, you know when to be quiet and when to talk when a younger girl shares her concerns.

- Share your experience to make the conversation more enlightening to the younger girl.

- Give useful tips on how to deal with mood swings, manage periods, or be more confident. Thankfully, you've learned all that.

- Encourage her to take care of herself and engage in activities that make her happy and relaxed.

- Celebrate her achievements and teach her how to handle setbacks.

- Be patient and lead by example. Show her, rather than tell her, how to deal with stress and emotions.

- Reassure her and be there for her. Be her safe space and let her know she can always come to you for help or to just talk.

- Share helpful resources such as this book to make it easier for her to understand periods.

By incorporating these practices into your life, you can build your confidence. This is essential in helping you navigate the challenges of puberty, accept yourself the way you are, achieve your goals, and learn to be a good mentor.

Carly Gross

Conclusion

You did it, girl!

You stayed with me until the end of this book—wow! That is so amazing. You should be proud of yourself for doing an awesome job. It was an exciting journey, and I hope it was exhilarating for you.

So far, you've gained important knowledge on how to embrace puberty and enjoy the experience. You've learned to be always connected with your body and appreciative of all it does to keep you strong. As you move forward, remember that embracing your body and its changes takes a conscious effort. But with a positive mindset, you can do whatever you set your mind to.

You will surely encounter challenges as you try to control and express your emotions healthily. There will be days when you do everything right, but it feels wrong. Don't give up! Everything takes time; you should not let your hard work be for nothing. Be confident and trust in your abilities!

Take care of your body and mind. Practice good hygiene, eat healthy meals, and improve your mindfulness practices. Be more creative and get enough rest. Don't be too hard on yourself during rough days. Instead, channel those feelings into something creative.

You are now equipped with a book on effectively handling your period, embracing your changes, managing your emotions, and being confident. Don't rush to finish using this book. You can always revisit it whenever you need to. Check in with your support group constantly, and always ask questions when confused. Be patient and celebrate your milestones.

Have you found this book helpful? Kindly share it with your friends. Your friends also need guidance on embracing changes and being more in tune with themselves during puberty. You can also leave a review so other girls can feel empowered.

Remember that your period is an experience you have to go through. Believe in yourself and know that you're never alone. You have a friend in this book.

Thank you for believing in this book and joining me on this journey. You're wonderful, and I'm excited about all the incredible things you will achieve as you grow older.

Keep shining bright!

A RESPECTFUL REQUEST

I hope you enjoyed reading this book.

If it made a positive impact on you, I would be so grateful if you could share your thoughts by leaving a **review on Amazon.**

Your review means a lot — it helps other readers discover the book and supports my journey as an independent author.

Even a few words about what you liked (or how it helped you) would be incredibly appreciated.

Scan the QR code below to review now!

Or simply visit:
www.bit.ly/review-periods

A Special FREE Gift Just for You

As a valued reader, we're excited to offer you 3 FREE books to make your growing-up journey easier and more comfortable.

What You'll Get:

1. **Growing Up Made Easy:** How to Handle Your First Period Like a Pro
2. **Period Self-Care Secrets:** How to Stay Happy, Healthy & Comfortable Every Month
3. **The Ultimate Period Cheat Sheet:** Fast Answers to Every Tween Girl's Questions

Scan the QR code below to download your free books instantly!

Or simply visit:
www.carlygross.com/gift-periods